£9.99

ADVANCED GEOGRAPHY Case Studies

MICHAEL HILL

D1347928

Hodder & Stoughton

A MEMBER

C257458

DEDICATION

To all those who explored and enjoyed these places with me

ACKNOWLEDGEMENTS

All photos provided by the author except for:
Figure 1.8 Norman Heal (Copyright Sally Reeve).

Special thanks to Rachel Rowe,
Librarian at the Royal Geographical Society for all her kind help.

Orders: please contact Bookpoint Ltd, 78 Milton Park, Abingdon, Oxon OX14 4TD. Telephone: (44) 01235 827720, Fax: (44) 01235 400454. Lines are open from 9.00–6.00, Monday to Saturday, with a 24 hour message answering service. Email address: orders@bookpoint.co.uk

British Library Cataloguing in Publication Data
A catalogue record for this title is available from The British Library

ISBN 0 340 71181 7

First published 1999
Impression number   10 9 8 7 6 5 4 3 2 1
Year   2005 2004 2003 2002 2001 2000 1999

Copyright © 1999 Michael Hill

Cover photos supplied by author.
Typeset by Multiplex Techniques Ltd, St. Mary Cray, Kent.
Printed in Great Britain for Hodder & Stoughton Educational, a division of Hodder Headline Plc,
338 Euston Road, London NW1 3BH by Redwood Books Ltd.

— ADVANCED CASE STUDIES —
CONTENTS

— ADVANCED CASE STUDIES

INTRODUCTION

A Level examiners frequently comment about the lack of detail given in examination answers where case studies are required. All too often the case study material is inappropriate, at the wrong scale or dealing with MEDCs rather than LEDCs, and vice versa. This book attempts to remedy some of these problems by providing the right amount of in-depth information on a wide range of systematic A Level topics, using regional, national and continental scales from different parts of the world. Different levels of economic development have also been taken into account, both with the balance between MEDCs and LEDCs and with the inclusion of case studies on Newly Industrialised Countries and Transition Economies.

The initial selection of the fifteen case studies was based upon a thorough analysis of the various syllabuses offered by the three main Examining Boards. The material will be equally relevant to the new courses which are being offered from the year 2000, when the A and AS Levels will undergo fairly radical changes; detailed case studies will remain an essential part of any advanced Geography course.

The first three case studies are on hydrological topics. The first considers river basin patterns and flooding on the regional scale in South West England, whilst the second is more concerned with the relationship between climate, river regimes and flooding in Japan, thus taking a national scale within an MEDC, before finally, the third takes an international scale with a group of LEDCs in the Middle East and North Africa, examining their water supplies and the potential conflicts between them; this is as much a study of economic resources as it is of the physical environment.

Case studies 4 and 5 are climatic and environmental. The first takes the continental scale of Africa and examines its broad climatic patterns as well as the ecosystems which they determine. The second looks in more detail at the national scale, using the regional variations in the climate of Spain. The African climatic study provides a background for the next case study, the rainforest of West Africa. This is considered at the West African regional level, yet at the same time focuses upon the national scale, with a more detailed look at Ghana. The other ecosystems case study in chapter 8 deals with soil erosion in one of Italy's poorest regions, Basilicata.

Case studies 8 and 9 deal with familiar topics – coasts and hazards, but use places which rarely appear in text books: Kent and Central America. Chapter 10 looks at all aspects of the demographic patterns in Peru, providing a detailed example on the national scale for an LEDC.

The two case studies on urban problems are based on Rome and Cairo; although both Mediterranean region cities, the former was selected to represent MEDC problems, latter to illustrate those of an LEDC. Singapore was selected as an example of an NIC, and although the case study concentrates on industrial development, it needs to be seen in the context of the broader framework of economic growth of the so-called 'Tiger Economies'. The rapid economic changes in Eastern Europe and the former USSR a illustrated in Case Study 14, which examines the state of the Baltic Republics. Fin the problems of tourism are examined in the last chapter, which focuses on Cent America, Costa Rica in particular and the concepts of ecotourism and sustainab

— CASE STUDY 1
RIVER BASINS AND FLOODING IN SOUTH WEST ENGLAND

More than any other environmental hazard, floods bring benefits as well as losses. They are a necessary part of most river ecosystems where they help to maintain wetland habitats.

Keith Smith, Environmental Hazards

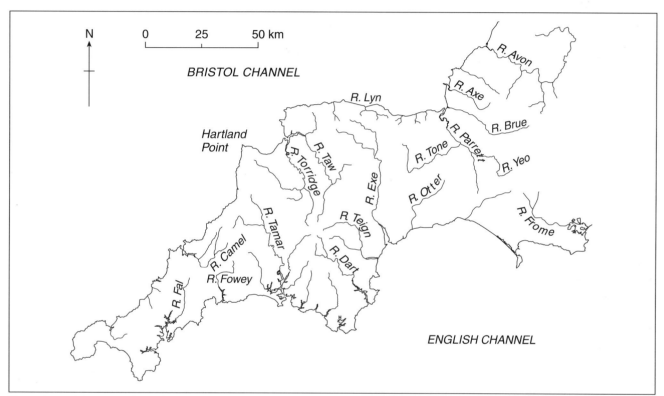

Figure 1.1 *Main rivers of South West England*

The South West Peninsula has a wide range of drainage basin patterns due to the diversity of its physical geography. Located on the Atlantic side of the British mainland, it has an above average rainfall and its rivers are liable to occasional spectacular flooding; indeed, the four most intensive rainfall events during the 20th century in England have all occurred in this region. By contrast, flooding may be regarded as a natural part of an annual cycle of events in certain areas of the South West, as in the Somerset Levels, where the height of the water table has brought controversy and conflict between farmers and conservationists. (Figure 1.1 shows the main river systems of the South West Peninsula.)

PHYSICAL BACKGROUND: RELIEF AND RAINFALL

The physique of the South West Peninsula is dominated by its uplands. (See Figure 1.2.) Through Cornwall and South Devon, the spine of the peninsula is formed by five granite bathyliths, which have gently rounded profiles broken by the occasional rocky tor; Dartmoor is the largest of these uplands and its summit, High Willhays (620 m) is the highest point in the South West. The upper parts of these 'moors' are covered with windswept heaths and the impermeability of their granite bedrock leaves large tracts of land sodden during the winter months. Seepage from these upland bogs and marshes is the main source of water for most of the rivers of the western part of the peninsula.

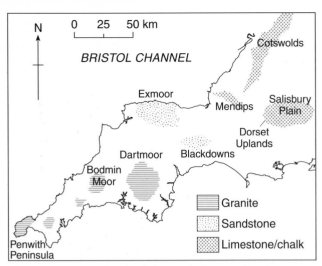

Figure 1.2 *Main uplands of the South West Peninsula*

Exmoor, the region's second largest upland straddles the Somerset–Devon border. It is composed of impermeable Old Red (Devonian) Sandstone, as are the neighbouring Brendon and Quantock Hills. Exmoor is the source of the region's most developed drainage system – that of the River Exe. In the north of the peninsula are the Mendips, a large anticline of Carboniferous Limestone which cuts across North Somerset from east to west. Here most of the drainage is underground and appears on the surface only where the underlying Old Red Sandstone is exposed.

Between the uplands lie areas of rolling countryside, well drained and well watered, with the rich soils that underpin the West Country's agricultural wealth. The Somerset Levels are the only extensive area of lowland in the South West. Once an inlet from the Bristol Channel, the sea has gradually receded from them, aided by human efforts to reclaim the land for agricultural use.

The South West Peninsula projects into the Atlantic, where it is exposed to the line of fire of mid-latitude depressions and the south-westerly winds with which they are associated. It therefore receives an annual rainfall of between 800 mm on the lowlands to over 2200 mm on the highest parts of Dartmoor. In certain years the rainfall is much higher making the South West more prone to extreme rainfall events than other parts of England. During the 20th century the following have been the most intense storms experienced in England:

Location	Intensity	Date
Martinstown, Dorset	279 mm/24 hrs	18.07.55
Bruton, Somerset	242 mm/24 hrs	28.06.17
Cannington, Somerset	238 mm/24 hrs	18.08.24
Simonsbath, Devon	231 mm/24 hrs	15.08.52

All of these records took place in the West Country and all occurred in the summer months as a result of heavy thunderstorms. The last of these was the cause of flooding off Exmoor which led to widespread damage at Lynmouth; in July 1968 a lower intensity (101 mm/24 hrs) thunderstorm over the Mendips was responsible for similarly spectacular flooding in Cheddar and other parts of North Somerset.

DRAINAGE BASINS

Relief, geology and rainfall patterns have all contributed to the South West's wide variety of drainage basin forms (see Figure 1.1). Parallel drainage patterns are found in two types of area:

1 where rivers are short, rising in uplands close to the sea
2 where rivers flow between parallel ridges of higher land.

There are thousands of small West Country rivers in the first category, including most Cornish rivers and the streams which drain from Exmoor into the Atlantic. Figure 1.3a shows a stretch of the Penwith Peninsula in West Cornwall which displays a parallel river system. Typically, in the South West these rivers have steep gradients and rocky beds, frequently interrupted by rapids and waterfalls, and therefore have the characteristics of mountain streams when they flow into the sea. Relative changes in sea level have led to rejuvenation of streams, particularly along the Atlantic coast of the region; near Hartland Point on the Devon-Cornwall border, Milford Water and Strawberry Water both have a sequence of several waterfalls just before they enter the sea, signifying either a relative rise in the land level, or rapid marine erosion that has left their valleys 'hanging' above the sea. The Somerset Levels exhibit the second type of parallel drainage; the rivers are much longer and have more tributaries than those further west, nevertheless the courses of the Rivers Parrett, Brue and Axe are forced to flow parallel to each other because of the trend of the higher lands of the Quantocks, Poldens and Mendips and the Isle of Wedmore (see Figure 1.9).

Parallel drainage patterns may eventually evolve into dendritic patterns through headward erosion and river capture, of which there is evidence in many parts of the South West, including the basin of the River Lyn and Strawberry Water, both in North Devon. The most developed examples of dendritic drainage patterns are to be found in the lower lying areas where long-term denudation has aided the

Figure 1.3 *Drainage patterns of the South West Peninsula*

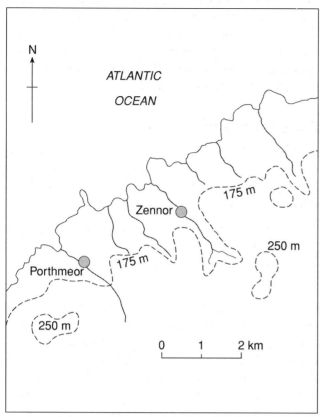

a *Parallel drainage on the Penwith Peninsula*

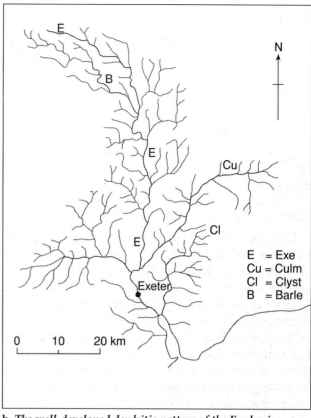

b *The well-developed dendritic pattern of the Exe basin*

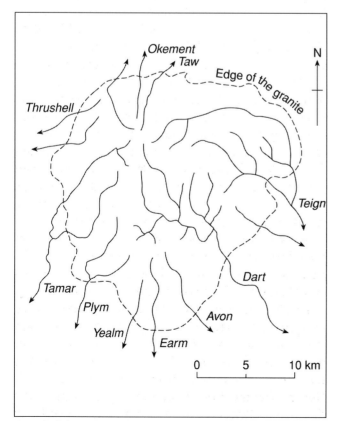

c *Radial drainage on Dartmoor*

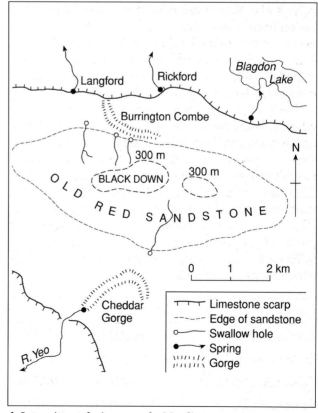

d *Intermittent drainage on the Mendips*

Figure 1.4 *A small parallel drainage channel (River Heddon)*

evolution of more complex systems. The River Exe (see Figure 1.3b), which rises close to the Bristol Channel yet drains into the English Channel, 85 km to the south, collects a large number of tributaries *en route* and consequently provides the best example of a well-developed dendritic drainage basin in the West Country. Other good examples of dendritic patterns are the Tamar, Taw and Torridge basins.

Radial patterns of drainage develop around the flanks of abruptly rising highlands surrounded by plains. The granite moorlands, which evolved as great bubbles of magma pushed up to form bathyliths, all have rivers draining radially from their summits. Dartmoor, the largest of the moorlands, has the most developed pattern (see Figure 1.3c).

The Mendips are the most extensive area of limestone in the South West. Their surface is incised by deep, dry gorges such as those at Cheddar and Burrington, which mark the courses of underground streams. Surface drainage is intermittent (see Figure 1.3d). There are small

surface streams flowing off the exposed impermeable strata of Old Red Sandstone, which form the summit of the Mendips, but these streams flow underground through swallow holes when they reach the Carboniferous Limestone. Their waters emerge through springs at the foot of the limestone anticline where they encounter impermeable strata.

RIVER AND BASIN CHARACTERISTICS

British rivers were the subject of a comprehensive study by the former National Environmental Research Council (NERC) which coordinated a detailed network of 1205 hydrometric gauging points in order to collect information about national hydrological patterns. Some of the characteristics of South West rivers are shown in Figure 1.5. (The basin areas to which the maps refer are shown in Figure 1.6.)

The drainage density map (Figure 1.5a) shows that densities are generally high in the South West, particularly in Cornwall and West Devon; this is a reflection of the impermeability of the granite and sandstones of the area. The rivers of such basin areas

Figure 1.5 *Drainage characteristics*

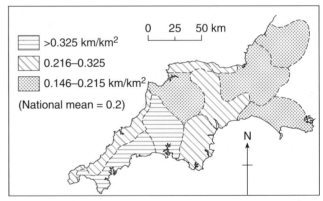

a *Drainage density*

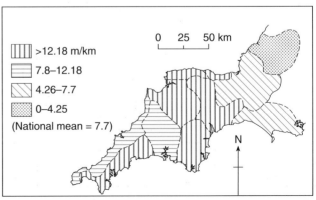

b *Mean channel slope*

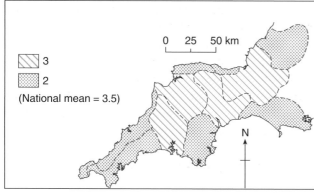

c *Order of largest stream*

are more liable to have a 'flashy' response to rainfall and a limited amount of baseflow because of their impermeable geology.

Each hydrological area has an above average number of river systems within it. This is both a reflection of drainage density and the way in which the shape and relief of the South West Peninsula have determined that most river systems will be short. Likewise, the mean channel slope is also greater than in much of Britain, and this reflects the abrupt nature of much of the relief of the South West, especially on the fringes of Dartmoor and Exmoor. Steep channel slopes are another indicator of a river's tendency to a flashy response to a rainstorm.

As rivers are fairly short in the South West, the longest being the Exe at just over 85 km, it is not surprising that the highest stream order of each area is fairly low. A clear distinction can be seen between those areas which are mainly coastal with shorter rivers and those which extend further inland.

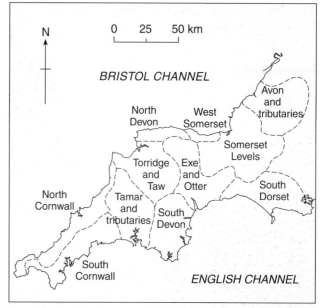

Figure 1.6 *Drainage areas of the South West Pennisula*

TWO WEST COUNTRY FLOODS

Two of the best documented floods in the West Country are those at Lynmouth in 1952 and the Mendips in 1968 and, although both were provoked by freak heavy summer storms, they provide a great hydrological contrast. The more localised, yet more devastating, Lynmouth flood was funnelled down from impermeable top of Exmoor through deep 'V'-shaped valleys; by contrast the Mendip flood which inundated numerous villages and towns, welled up from the depths of the limestone and caused normally dry valleys to run as torrents. Figure 1.7

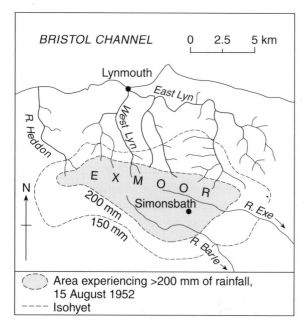

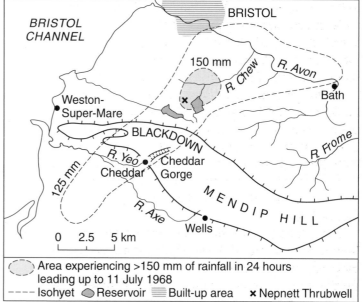

Figure 1.7 *Two contrasting West Country floods*

Figure 1.8 *Archive photo of the 1968 flood (Cheddar Gorge)*

locates the two areas and shows the rainfall patterns which caused their floods.

The Lynmouth flood was mainly the result of antecedent rainfall. The first fortnight of August 1952 had seen heavy rainfall throughout the South West; this led to the saturation of the soils on the moorland summit of Exmoor. Then, on 15 August, one of the heaviest downpours ever recorded in Britain fell on the top of Exmoor; the 220 mm plus rainfall which fell over a large area surrounding the summit of Exmoor was quickly channelled into the tributaries which feed the East and West Lyn rivers. This created a flood surge which was funnelled down through the narrow valleys to inundate the town at the river's mouth.

The flood surge carried huge boulders and uprooted trees with it, but the artificial structures such as flood prevention walls within Lynmouth made matters worse by further concentrating the water flow; bridges, especially that over the West Lyn, in the centre of the town acted as barriers behind which water and debris ponded up before bursting out in the form of a tidal wave.

The toll of damage was high for a British flood; 34 people lost their lives, of which 11 were holidaymakers, 90 houses were destroyed or had to

be demolished because of being rendered unsafe, 130 cars were destroyed and 19 boats were lost at sea. Lynmouth was sealed off for three weeks as reconstruction work started; a workforce of 1000 was deployed by the army to help in the operations. Repairs to the town, which included new, wider bridges and channel walls were completed within 2½ years. The most permanent reminder of the flood is the large pebble delta which was formed at the mouth of the River Lyn, remarkable for both the size of the deposits and that it has been created in a sea area with such a high tidal range.

The 'great flood' of the Mendips which occurred in July 1968, was of a very different nature. There were fewer fatalities – only seven people died, but damage was caused over a much wider area, as the thunderstorm which caused the flood worked its way north-eastwards. On the top of the Mendips, as with Exmoor, there was considerable antecedent moisture in the soil, which was already saturated when the main rainfall event occurred, thereby preventing any further infiltration. An unusually intense thunderstorm led to the fall of 131 mm of rain in 24 hours on the top of Black Down, which at its peak registered 69 mm per hour; the highest rainfall in the area was, however, at the village of Nempnett Thrubwell on the northern slopes of the Mendips, where 171 mm fell during 24 hours. The peak rainfall was at 10 p.m. on 10 July.

Water reached the rivers of the area both from underground, rising up through the limestone, and across the saturated surfaces. The River Yeo in Cheddar is fed from underground sources flowing beneath the Cheddar Gorge. Its average rate of discharge is normally a mere 0.94 cumecs from baseflow. The stormflow from 10 – 11 July added to this eleven fold. On the northern flanks of the Mendips the spring-fed Langford stream increased its flow sixteen fold.

Flooding occurred in all the rivers which radiate off the Mendips, but the most dramatic storm surge was that which filled Cheddar Gorge. Normally a dry valley, it became a raging torrent of load-charged water. As with the Lynmouth flood, artificial structures made matters worse; the roads across dry valleys on the top of the Mendips caused flood-water to pond up and become more dangerous once the barriers were breached.

The flood surge through Cheddar tore up the road in the Gorge, depositing boulders in its path, destroying cars and inundating scores of homes, leaving behind muddy deposits. Thirty-five people

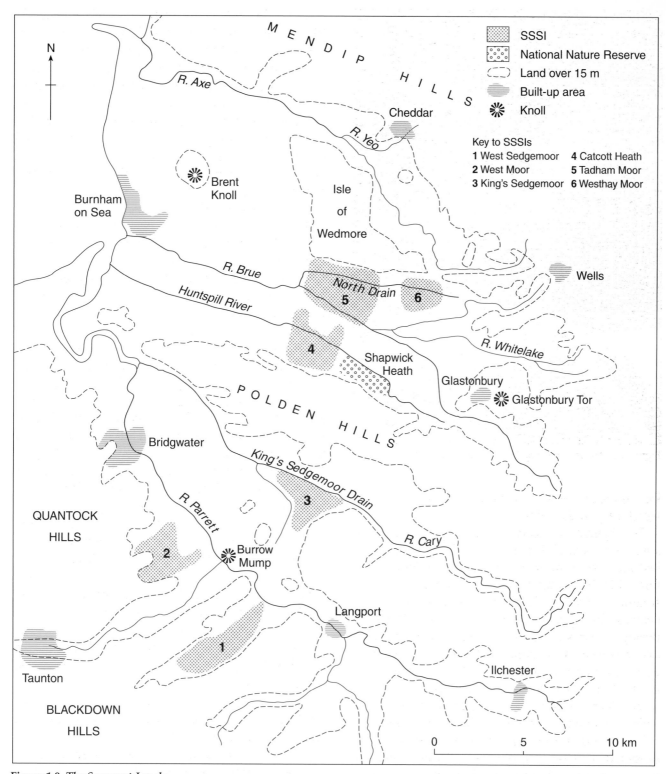

Figure 1.9 *The Somerset Levels*

needed to be rehoused and one farmer lost 40 000 chickens. The tourist centre of Cheddar was closed for two weeks while repairs were carried out.

The effects of the flood were widespread throughout the north of Somerset. Sixty-seven bridges were destroyed in the county, Weston-Super-Mare was cut off by landslides and the village of Pensford, near Bath, experienced a 3 m tidal wave.

Underground in the limestone caverns that criss-cross the Mendips, cavers found even more damage than on the surface, with new passageways opened up and old ones closed by the rubble carried in the sub-

river basins and flooding in South West England

Figure 1.10 *Part of the Somerset Levels*

surface turbulence of the flood-waters. After the flood there was much debate about the frequency of the occurrence of storms and floods of this magnitude. Estimates from various hydrologists varied between a 120-year recurrence and a 100 000-year recurrence. No doubt the truth lies somewhere in between, but it does illustrate how, where the evidence is scanty, it is difficult to make useful or accurate predictions.

THE SOMERSET LEVELS

The low-lying zone of central Somerset, which stretches from Wells to Taunton known as the Somerset Moors or Levels, is an area in which flooding was traditionally part of the rural economy. Once a vast area of shallow lakes and marshes punctuated by ridges of hills and isolated knolls, it gained its present form from the land drainage schemes which reached a peak of activity between 1770 and 1840, at the time of the Acts of Enclosure.

The Levels afford a flat, green landscape cut across by a chequerboard of artificial drainage ditches or 'rhynes' which are lined by rows of pollarded willows. The rhynes drain into the main rivers of the region which are straightened and embanked in order to prevent excessive flooding. As a result of reclamation, the land has shrunk and much of the farmland lies below the level of the major rivers such as the Brue and the Parrett; this has obviated a network of sluices and pumping stations to control water movement from rhynes to rivers, as well as from rivers to the sea. The lowest land, which is underlain by peat, is found in the

centre of the Levels on Westhay Moor, south of the Isle of Wedmore, where the average height above sea level is just 3 m. The zone closer to the sea is underlain by clay and is slightly more elevated (approximately 6 m), which has been one of the contributory factors to the seasonal flooding of the past. The high tidal range of the Bristol Channel (13 m during spring tides) is yet another problem for drainage of the area.

The Levels, which cover some 400 km², were, and still are, an area predominantly engaged in dairy farming; cattle were traditionally grazed on the rich meadows of the lowest land in summer and taken to the higher fields during the winter floods. The growing of 'withy' (willow) stems for basket making, the extraction of peat (once for fuel but now for sale in garden centres) and the production of cider apples have all been important elements in the rural economy for a long time. The seasonal winter flooding of the most low-lying areas was taken as part of the annual cycle of events within the framework of which the local people lived and worked.

The intensification of farming in the 1960s and 1970s led to changes and conflicts within the Somerset Levels. In places, pasture land was given over to crops such as cereals, and farmers were keen to lower the water table and create more efficient drainage; at the same time there was widespread use of artificial fertilisers in areas where they had never been put before. Interest in the wildlife of the Somerset Levels was also intensifying at this time, as scientists and conservationists realised the threat to what is perhaps Britain's most biodiverse wetland environment. In 1977 this was recognised by the Nature Conservancy, when it published *The Somerset Wetlands Project* which stressed the need for conservation of this unique ecosystem.

The unimproved meadows may have 100 flower species per field, including rare orchids, the rhynes are varied hydrosere habitats, 22 butterfly species inhabit the area and, most important, the hugh population of breeding and wintering birds visit these wetlands. The decline in the number of species as a result of new farming practices led to action from the Royal Society for the Protection of Birds (RSPB) and other environmentalists. Six areas became SSSIs and a National Nature Reserve was set up at Shapwick Heath. In 1981 there was well-above-average rainfall which caused widespread flooding, increasing local farmers' desires to create more efficient drainage which would have led to a lowering the water table.

The conflicts between farmers and conservationists reached a peak in 1983, the year in which West Sedgemoor, the most contested area, became an SSSI. The farmers staged what became known as their 'pitchfork rebellion' (named after the Monmouth Rebellion which took place in the area 298 years earlier). It involved the farmers deliberately breaking the newly imposed rules concerning protected land and the ritual burning of effigies of the conservationists.

A compromise was eventually reached and farmers were given compensation to be persuaded to cooperate with the government and accept the new status of the land. In the more recent age of 'set-aside', pressure for intensification of land use has subsided. Growth industries in the area such as tourism and recreation are where farmers may now be able to diversify their incomes and, at the same time, preserve the Somerset Levels in their traditional state.

SUMMARY

- ● South West has the biggest concentration of freak storms in Britain
- ● High relief intercepts SW prevailing winds
- ● Rainfall reaches 2200 mm on Dartmoor
- ● High drainage density
- ● Low stream orders
- ● Steep relief in much of the peninsula
- ● Good examples of parallel, radial, dendritic and intermittent drainage
- ● Lynmouth flood 1952, heavy runoff from Exmoor
- ● Mendip flood of 1968 from surface runoff and groundwater
- ● Somerset Levels artificially drained
- ● Flooding part of traditional economy
- ● Conflicts between farmers and conservationists

 EXAMINATION QUESTIONS

This case study is of relevance to questions on drainage basins, flooding and the hydrological cycle in general. The case study also relates to Hazards and the Somerset Levels section relates to Ecosystems sections of the syllabus.

SPECIFIC

Examples of questions which make direct use of the case study:

1 With reference to examples you have studied, examine the causes and consequences of river floods.

2 With reference to an area you have studied, outline the main physical factors responsible for flooding.

GENERAL

More general use of the case study in combination with others could be:

3 Examine the conflicts which may arise in land use within one or more ecosystems which you have studied.

4 Using any two different natural hazards you have studied and, illustrating your answer with specific examples, examine the impact they may have upon human activity.

— CASE STUDY — ② RIVER REGIMES AND FLOODING IN JAPAN

> **For a country of its size, Japan has remarkable diversity in its river regimes. The multiplicity of sources which supply these rivers is for the most part the reason for such diversity.**
>
> *René Frécaut*

Japan is both a relatively small country (with a total area of 377 815 km²), and a mountainous one. Given these two factors, its river basins are generally limited in size and their courses flow over short distances from their mountain sources in the centre of the country to the seas which surround it. (Figure 2.1 shows the main rivers of Japan.)

The annual average rainfall in Japan is high, as most parts of the country receive well over 1000 mm per year; this, together with the seasonal variations in the patterns of precipitation between north and south and between places along the Sea of Japan and those along the Pacific Ocean, means that the country has considerable variations in its river regimes.

Japan's climate can be erratic and there may, therefore, be large variations in precipitation between one year and the next, and even between decades. Floods may occur suddenly and, although generally seasonal, the actual month of maximum flow will vary from year to year. The summer typhoon season is that most closely associated with flood disasters, especially in the more subtropical parts of the archipelago.

High levels of urbanisation, industrialisation and the dependency upon the hydrologically demanding staple of rice, all mean that Japan's rivers are heavily exploited and, therefore, controlled. Industrial and domestic water supply needs have led to widespread damming of rivers, and this is frequently combined with the production of hydroelectricity. On the plains, in particular, rivers have been tamed for hundreds of years for the irrigation of the rice paddies, by the creation of intricate networks of canals.

RAINFALL PATTERNS

Japan's position in the Pacific Ocean on the edge of the Eurasian landmass, makes it a zone of conflict between continental and oceanic airmasses of both tropical and polar origins. Winters are dominated by the north-westerlies blowing from the cold continental interior, whereas summers are influenced by the tropical south-easterlies coming in from the Pacific. Interspersed with these major seasons are four shorter ones, giving Japan a total of six seasons. Each seasonal period has its own particular rainfall pattern, but owing to topography, aspect and the distribution of land and sea, different parts of Japan are affected in different ways. Overall, Japan receives more rainfall in the summer months than in the winter, the opposite situation from all Mediterranean countries which although located at similar latitudes, are on the west coasts of the continents.

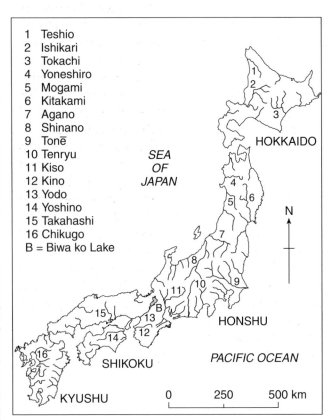

1   Teshio
2   Ishikari
3   Tokachi
4   Yoneshiro
5   Mogami
6   Kitakami
7   Agano
8   Shinano
9   Tonē
10 Tenryu
11 Kiso
12 Kino
13 Yodo
14 Yoshino
15 Takahashi
16 Chikugo
B = Biwa ko Lake

Figure 2.1 *The main rivers of Japan*

The six seasons may be summarised as follows:

1   **Winter monsoon**. (December to February) This is the longest wet season with rain and snow brought by the north-westerlies from the continental landmass, interspersed with clear, dry, anticyclonic weather. Snow falls on the Central Alps of Honshu and widely throughout Hokkaido; further south the precipitation is mainly in the form of rain. The western side of Japan has higher precipitation levels during this period than the east, which remains in the rain shadow.

2   **Spring**. (March to early June, or late June in Hokkaido and Northern Honshu) Spring is a period of transition from the dominance of continental influences to that of the tropical maritime airmasses. Spring is drier that winter, but can be unsettled.

3   *Baiu*. (Late June to mid July) *Baiu* is a period of heavy rainstorms which marks the north-westerly movement of the polar front over Japan, when tropical and continental airmasses come into contact, leading to numerous depressions. The Pacific coast receives heavier rainfall than the north coast.

4   **Midsummer**. (Late July and August) Midsummer is a very hot and humid season, which is normally dry, apart from irregular thunderstorms and the occasional typhoon.

5   *Shurin*. (September to early October) *Shurin* is another rainy season associated with the return of the polar front as it crosses Japan in a south-easterly direction, to return to its winter position over the Eurasian landmass.

6   **Autumn** (Late October to late November) Autumn is often the most stable and driest time of year with long periods of anticyclone.

From the above list of seasons, it can be appreciated why Japan has a high average rainfall and also why there is likely to be considerable variation in the pattern of river regimes through the archipelago. The typhoon season still further complicates the situation, as this period, during which anything between 3 and 30 tropical cyclones may hit Japan, can last from June until November. In particularly wet years, such as 1993, the various summer seasons and the coming of the typhoons may merge and blend into an almost continuously rainy summer from June until September. On such occasions flooding will be much more widespread than usual. (Figure 2.2 shows the annual total distribution of rainfall in Japan.)

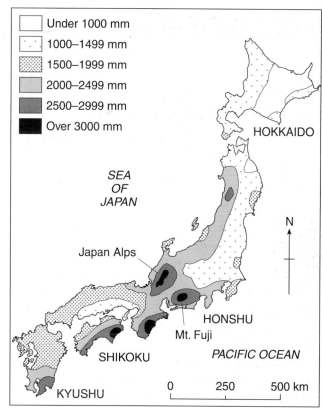

Figure 2.2 *Annual rainfall totals of Japan*

TOPOGRAPHY AND RIVER BASINS

With 74 per cent of its terrain classified as mountainous, most of Japan's river basins are hemmed in by rugged topography and are relatively ill-developed. In many places, such as the northern coast of Honshu, where the mountain spines are close to the sea, rivers tend to form into parallel drainage patterns. Only where there are extensive plains, such as in the Kanto region to the north of Tokyo, are basin patterns much more complex.

For most rivers, coastal plains and flood plains account for only between 10 per cent and 30 per cent of their total course lengths. Only three Japanese rivers reach over 300 km in length; the longest being the Shinano (369 km) which rises in the central mountains of Honshu and flows out into the Sea of Japan at Niigata. The Ishikari (365 km) is the longest river on Hokkaido Island and the second longest in Japan. The Tonē (322 km), although only the third in length, is in many ways Japan's most important river; it not only drains much of the Kanto Plain, but with a total area of 16 840 km², has the largest drainage basin in the country.

RIVER REGIMES OF JAPAN

Every Japanese river has its own characteristic flow pattern and is in that sense unique; nevertheless, similarities can be found between rivers within each region of the country, enabling distinctive river regimes to be identified. Japan can clearly be divided into five divisions, each with river regimes relating to regional climate and topography. These regions, which are shown on Figure 2.3, are as follows:

1 **Cold Temperate Zone**. (Hokkaido) Being the most northerly of Japan's main islands, Hokkaido experiences some of the most severe winters in the archipelago. River regimes on this island are dominated by spring snowmelt, rather than any major input from rainfall. Hokkaido is too far north to be strongly influenced by heavy rains in the various summer seasons. Rivers such as the Ishikari, therefore, tend to have one large, dramatic discharge peak during April.

2 **Cool Temperate Zone**. (Northern Honshu) Regimes in this part of Japan are influenced by spring snowmelt as well as certain rainy seasons. This gives rivers within the area three discharge peaks, the first and largest coinciding with April snowmelt, the other two reflecting

pluvial seasons. Rivers draining to the north coast (e.g. Mogami) are influenced by both the *baiu* and the winter monsoon, whereas those draining to the Pacific Ocean (e.g. Kitakami) are influenced by the *baiu* and *shurin* rainy seasons.

Figure 2.4 *Waterfalls on the upper course of a river in the Japan Alps*

3 **High Mountain Zone**. (Central Highlands of Honshu) Regimes in this zone are dominated by the highest winter snowfall in Japan, together with high levels of rainfall throughout most of the rest of the year. Rivers which flow mainly through the Japanese Alps and the other spinal regions of Honshu include the Shinano and Agano. Both rivers have two main discharge maxima, from spring snowmelt and *baiu* rains. There is a slight tendency towards a third maximum in late summer, but these rivers are effectively within the rain shadow of the maritime north-easterlies.

4 **Subtropical Eastern Zone**. (South Eastern Honshu) Rivers within this zone are still influenced to some extent by snowmelt from the mountains of central Honshu, but rainfall plays a much more important role in their flow patterns. Rivers may either have two maxima (e.g. the Tonē, with its lower maximum in spring from snowmelt and a higher maximum in June from the *baiu* rains) or three maxima (e.g. the Kiso, from winter monsoon, *baiu* and *shurin* rains).

5 **Subtropical Western Zone**. (Western Honshu, Shikoku and Kyushu) These regimes are fed entirely from rainfall and rivers within the zone and have two distinctive maxima, relating to the *baiu* and *shurin* rains (e.g. Chikugo and Yoshino Rivers). However, as these are the most likely rivers to be influenced by tropical typhoons,

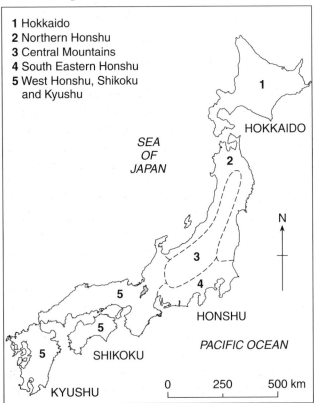

1 Hokkaido
2 Northern Honshu
3 Central Mountains
4 South Eastern Honshu
5 West Honshu, Shikoku and Kyushu

SEA OF JAPAN

HOKKAIDO

N

HONSHU

PACIFIC OCEAN

SHIKOKU

KYUSHU

0   250   500 km

Figure 2.3 *River regimes of Japan*

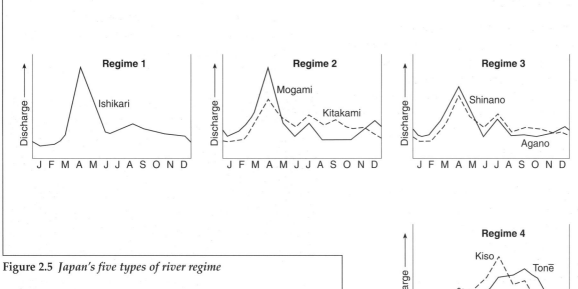

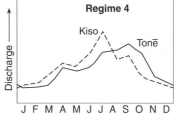

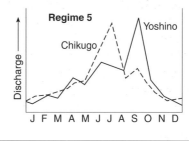

Figure 2.5 *Japan's five types of river regime*

individual annual flow patterns can vary greatly from the long-term regime patterns. Figure 2.5 shows the regime flow patterns for each of the five distinctive zones.

The unpredictable nature of the rainy seasons in Japan (they may arrive early or late, and within the June to November period typhoons occur at irregular intervals) means that rivers do not necessarily have their maximum flows at the same time each year.

Studies have been carried out on a number of rivers to analyse their inter-annual variations which effectively show deviations from the normal regime patterns. The River Ishikari in Hokkaido was studied over a 13-year period; it was shown that its main snowmelt-generated maximum occurred in April of 11 occasions and in May just twice. The secondary maximum, associated with the *shurin* rains was more variable as it occurred once in July, nine times in August and three times in September. This study shows the greater reliability of the snowmelt imput, *vis à vis* that from the summer rains.

An even more detailed survey was carried out on the Tone over a 28-year period. The two maxima of the Tone vary even more than those of the Ishikari. The main maximum is that associated with the *shurin* rains; on six occasions this occurred in July, five times in August, ten times in September and six times in October. The secondary maximum is that associated with spring snowmelt; on 19 occasions this fell in April and on 8 occasions during May. In one of the years of this particular study, the whole pattern was reversed, coinciding with an especially cold winter; the spring snowmelt produced the

main maximum and the summer rains the secondary maximum.

With such irregularities in their flow patterns, the rivers of Japan are very much subject to localised flooding. Individual measurements of maximum flows are difficult to compare between one river to the next as basin sizes vary so much. Figure 2.5, however, shows the adjusted statistics for river flows, taking basin size into account. From this graph it can be clearly seen that the Agano and Tone are the most 'flashy' of the ten rivers, as they display the highest flows per square kilometre. Both these rivers have complex tributary networks and have sources in the high mountain areas of Central Honshu; these two factors go a long way towards explaining the unpredictable nature of their discharge patterns. The lowest two figures are those of the Yodo and Chikugo; neither river rises in high mountains and both have fairly limited numbers of tributaries. However, they are still both suseptible to unpredictable flooding as they are both in the direct firing line of typhoon-generated rains.

Area	Litres per second per km
Ishikari	370
Mogami	400
Kitikami	475
Shinano	650
Agano	1300
Tonē	1250
Kiso	120
Yodo	75
Yoshino	250
Chikugo	180

Figure 2.6 *Maximum river flows per unit area*

Not only does the discharge of Japanese rivers vary greatly with season, but also their load. Snowmelt brings with it eroded materials from the mountains together with weathered materials which have accumulated upon and within the snowbeds throughout the winter. The seasonal high discharge from snowmelt also increases the rivers' erosive capacity as meltwater moves downstream. Similarly, during the periods of flooding triggered off by summer rains, erosion rates are much higher within the river channels; this increase in load is further added to by material from landslides which are especially common in the more subtropical parts of Japan.

THE RIVER TONĒ

The Tonē-gawa (Tonē River), with a drainage area of 16 840 km^2, is the largest river basin in Japan; it is also the most important river system crossing the Kanto Plain, Japan's largest continous area of flat land (see Figure 2.7). Like other Japanese rivers, it flows through three distinctive types of landscape: the mountain zone, the diluvial zone at the foot of the mountains where coarse gravel deposits have accumulated, and the broader, more open alluvial plains upon which much finer deposits are laid down, particularly when rivers are in flood.

Where the Tonē and its various tributaries have their headwaters, high in the mountains of Central Honshu, the valleys are narrow, rocky, steep-sided with frequent breaks in their long profiles where waterfalls cross localised areas of more resistant geology such as old lava flows. Tectonic activity associated with Japan's young fold mountains and

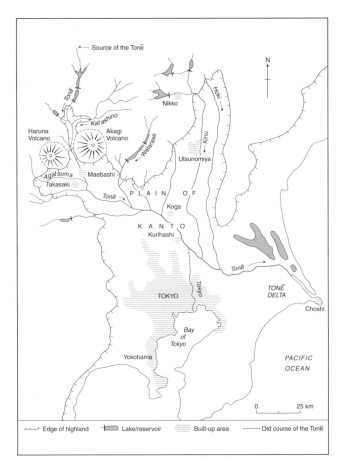

Figure 2.7 *The Tonē basin and Kanto Plain*

recent volcanic activity, has led to considerable entrenchment of the upper courses of the Tonē and its tributaries. Some of these mountain stretches of river valley have become completely altered by human developments; Japan's high density of population together with its shortage of fossil fuels have led to the development of multipurpose reservoirs with their associated hydroelectricity plants. The nature of the terrain has tended to encourage many small developments rather than large-scale 'megadams'.

Figure 2.8 *The Tonē at low flow with fishermen*

Nowhere in the upper catchment area of the Tonē basin is more altered, engineered and, therefore, scenically degraded, than the headwaters of the Watarase tributary where a series of reservoirs, power stations, sawmills and mines give it a character reminiscent of South Wales in the early 20th century. The headwaters of the Tonē itself are also highly developed with dams and reservoirs, but by no means as industrialised. With increased pressure upon the natural resources and environment, more valleys are flooded for hydroelectric production, the most recent of which taking place during the late 1990s and has involved the drowning of the beautiful gorges and waterfalls of the Agatsuma river valley. One of the reasons for the large number of hydroelectricity plants in Japan is the very erratic and seasonal nature of the rainfall, which can make individual power stations rather unreliable in their output.

As the River Tonē flows down through its restricted valley between the Akagi and Haruna volcanoes, it enters its diluvial plain. Here the river becomes much wider, is heavily braided because of the amount of gravel which is brought down annually from the mountains, and is more liable to large fluctuations in its flow pattern. Maebashi, with a population of 350 000, the largest city on the Tonē is located at this strategic point. Capital of the prefecture of Gunma and formerly the headquarters of a *samurai* warlord, Maebashi developed as an important centre of serriculture and the textile industry.

The city is always at the mercy of the huge fluctuations in the Tonē's flow. One day the river may be crystal clear with numerous lampshade-hatted fishermen wading in the gravel-strewn shallows and hooking out trout; the next the muddy, swirling waters may be more than 5 m higher and carrying uprooted trees from the mountains upstream. All along the banks of the Tonē in Maebashi is evidence of various flood prevention schemes, levees, gabions, revetments, concrete walls, boulders, tetrapods many of them destroyed or rendered useless by the floods, some even left on newly created islands in the ever changing braided course of the river. In the end the river seems to win, whatever the method of flood protection.

Sensibly, most housing and other buildings are located on the gravel terraces high above normal flood levels; however, 100-year or 200-year floods are still likely to create disasters, such as that in the mid-18th century, which altered the river's course so drastically that it swept the *samurai* castle downstream.

Figure 2.9 *Tetrapods used to reinforce the banks of the River Tonē*

Maebashi and its neighbouring towns are located on the densely populated Kanto Plain, for which the Tonē and its tributaries are a source of life particularly for the cultivation of rice and other crops. The countryside is intricately subdivided into small plots for rice paddies and the level of localised hydraulic engineering is very complex. Few other river valley landscapes in the world can be as altered and controlled as that of the Kanto Plain.

At Kurihashi the Tonē is very broad and still heavily braided, but at this point it has passed from its diluvial stage to the alluvial section of its course. Here, research has been carried out into both the recent flow patterns of the Tonē and how the river flowed in the past. In a study which took place over a 28-year period, it was found that the River Tonē,

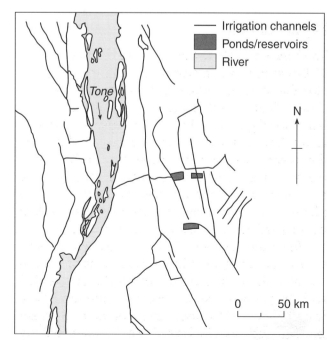

Figure 2.10 *The Tonē in the northern suburbs of Maebashi*

with a normal flow of about 500 cumecs, went to over 2000 cumecs on 21 occasions, over 3000 cumecs on 15 occasions, 4000 cumecs 12 times, over 5000 cumecs on 8 occasions and over 7000 cumecs 7 times. The most extreme flood events were those coinciding with typhoons; nevertheless, the figures illustrate the highly variable nature of the Tonē. Even further evidence can be found in the past deposits laid down by the Tonē at Kurihashi.

The Tonē originally flowed out into the Bay of Tokyo, roughly where the Edo or Tokyo River enters the Bay today. It was the extremely 'flashy' nature of the river which caused the hydraulic engineers to divert its course in 1654 in order to let it flow out into the Pacific Ocean through the less populated area to the north of Tokyo. In the intervening centuries the Tonē has built up a very large cuspate delta, once again evidence of its great power to erode and deposit, particularly when in spate.

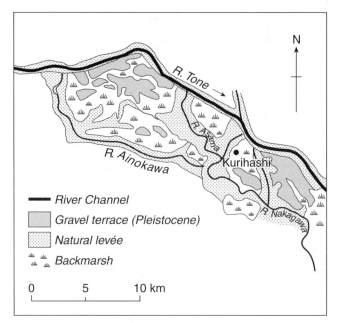

Figure 2.11 *Part of the Tonē Plain near Kurihashi*

SUMMARY

- Japan is small and mountainous
- High rainfall throughout the country
- Marked seasonality of the rains
- Six seasons
- Longest river, Shinano at 369 km
- Biggest basin, the Tonē at 16 840 km²
- Five categories of river regimes
- Most Japanese rivers have flashy regimes
- The upper courses of Japanese rivers tend to be highly altered

---

EXAMINATION QUESTIONS

This case study deals with river basins, river regimes and flooding and, therefore, has relevance to a wide range of hydrological questions.

SPECIFIC

An example of questions which make direct use of this case study:

1 With reference to a country or region you have studied, explain why rivers may vary considerably in their annual flood patterns.

Less specific and more challenging are questions such as:

2 Why are some rivers more likely to flood than others?

GENERAL

The more general use of this case study, which could be in conjunction with examples from other parts of the world could be:

3 Examine the relationships between human activity and the various parts of the hydrological cycle.

Japan is frequently studied as an example of a hazardous environment, and information from this study could be used to help illustrate a question such as:

4 With reference to a country you have studied, examine why it has a hazardous environment and what impact this has upon the country's people.

— CASE STUDY — ③
WATER RESOURCE CONFLICTS IN THE MIDDLE EAST

> **The one certainty in the Middle East today is that water has become a commodity as important as oil: to those who possess it, it is a means of leverage and a way of protecting power; to those which lack supplies, a prime concern of national security must be to increase what is available.**
>
> Bulloch and Darwish, *Water Wars*

Eighty per cent of the Middle East can be classified as arid. With the exception of some high mountain areas (e.g. the Elburz in Iran), there are few places where low temperatures act as a restraint upon agriculture and other forms of human activity; however, water supply, both in terms of annual total and seasonal distribution, is absolutely critical. Figure 3.1 shows the rainfall totals for various cities in the region, together with the 100mm and 500mm isohyets. The areas with the highest rainfall are generally found around the periphery of the region (e.g. the Atlas Mountains and the Caspian and Black Sea coasts).

Not only is there a problem with low rainfall, but also high evapotranspiration rates; July temperatures in the Middle East are very high, which is advantageous for crop growth only if there is sufficent water supply. Some examples of average July temperatures are:

Tripoli 25 °C;   Beirut 27 °C;   Tehran 29 °C;
Baghdad 33 °C;   Riyadh 35 °C.

The four water-balance graphs for Tripoli, Cairo, Beirut and Baghdad (Figure 3.2), indicate just how important irrigation is to compensate for the water deficiency in the region.

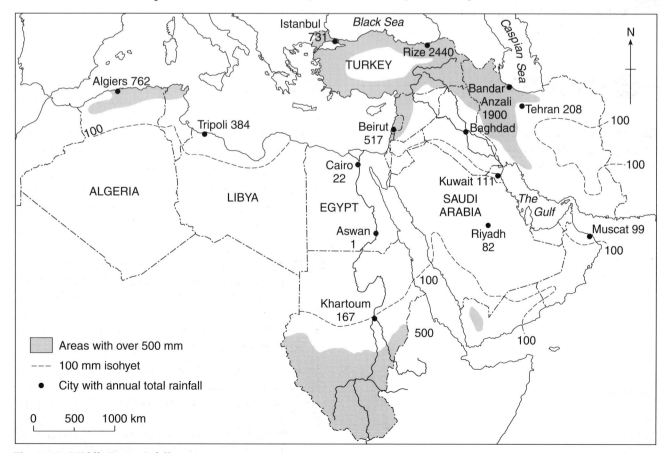

Figure 3.1 *Middle East rainfall*

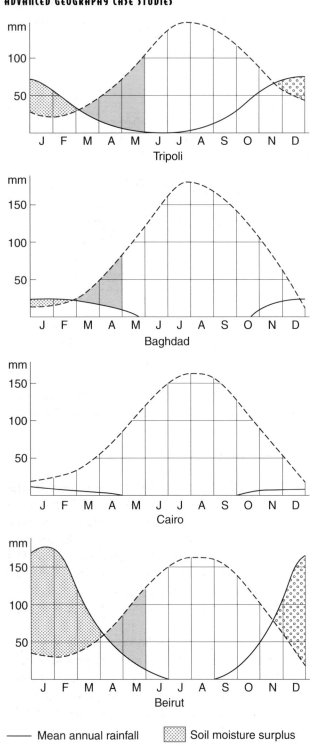

— Mean annual rainfall

- - - Mean annual potential
evapotranspiration

[dotted] Soil moisture surplus

[grey] Soil moisture utilisation

[white] Soil moisture defecit

[circles] Soil moisture recharge

Figure 3.2 *Water balances for four Middle Eastern cities*

THE SOURCES OF WATER

There are six main sources of fresh water in the Middle East.

1 **The larger perennial rivers**. These are exogenous to the arid zone, rising in mountains and other high rainfall areas beyond the desert fringes. Only three rivers fit into this category: the Tigris and Euphrates, which rise in the mountains of Anatolian Turkey, and the Nile with its twin sources in the Ethiopian Highlands and the savanna lands of East Africa.

2 **Smaller perennial rivers** such as the Jordan, Orontes and Litani which, although they have a comparatively low discharge, are crucial for life in the areas through which they flow.

3 **Wadis**. There are thousands of dry river beds throughout the Middle East: those which flow with water occasionally or seasonally may be dammed to catch the valuable extra water supplies they provide. Saudi Arabia is, at present, building more than 60 of these catchment dams.

4 **Shallow aquifers**. These groundwater sources are associated with the various hills and uplands formed from sedimentary rocks (e.g. the Lebanon ranges and the Jebel Akhdar in Oman). Such aquifers are recharged naturally from local seasonal rains and consequently can be regarded as a long-term resource, if they are not over-exploited. Unfortunately, in many coastal places the lowering of the water table in these aquifers is causing saltwater contamination.

5 **Deep fossil water aquifers**. Across the region are huge underground supplies of water which have been lodged in artesian basins and other geological structures for over 10 000 years, since the end of the last Ice Age, (see Figure 3.3). Despite their size, these should not be regarded as limitless or renewable, as the climate of the region is now much drier than it was when they were formed. Moreover, many deep aquifers already exploited have proved to contain brackish rather than fresh water.

6 **Desalination plants**. A long-term solution to the water shortage must be the desalination of seawater. At the moment this is still an expensive alternative to using freshwater supplies and is operated only by the more wealthy countries, especially those which are oil-rich. (See Figure 3.3). Solar energy is abundant in the Middle East and could prove to be the best power source for desalination, when a sufficiently cheap form of technology is developed.

The two largest sources of water, the major perennial rivers and the deep fossil groundwater,

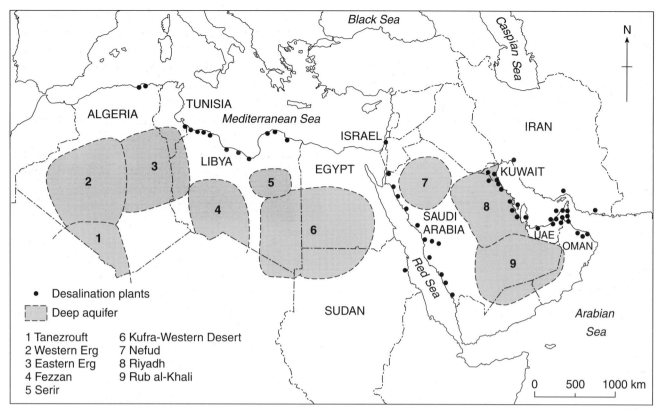

Figure 3.3 *Deep fossil aquifers of the Sahara and Arabia; Distribution of main desalination plants*

cross international boundaries and have become the subjects of friction between countries and could be the possible causes of future wars in the Middle East. Population growth rates are high in the region (see Figure 3.4), and as the number of people continues to increase, water supplies will become even more precious.

Country	Population (millions)	Growth rate (% p.a.)	Doubling time (years)	Population in 2025 (millions)
Egypt	64.8	2.1	34	97.7
Libya	5.6	3.6	19	14.4
Sudan	27.9	2.1	33	46.9
Iraq	21.2	2.8	25	42.4
Iran	67.5	2.7	26	111.9
Israel	5.8	1.5	47	8.0
Turkey	63.7	1.6	43	89.9
Syria	15.0	2.8	25	26.3
Jordan	4.4	3.3	21	8.5
Saudi Arabia	19.5	3.1	23	42.4

Figure 3.4 *Population statistics for selected middle eastern countries*

THE RIVER NILE

The Nile, at 6825 km, is the longest river in the world. Its basin covers 2.9 million km², 10 per cent of the area of Africa. Although it influences nine countries, three in particular, Egypt, Sudan and Ethiopia, are very dependent upon its waters. The source of the Blue Nile is in Ethiopia, and the White Nile flows through Sudan where it is joined by numerous tributaries in the swampy Sudd region. (See Figure 3.5).

'Egypt is the gift of the Nile' is an old saying – and, indeed, the 64 million people of this desert state would not exist without it. At present, Egypt controls the waters of the Nile, a major exception to the general rule that upstream states are normally the regulators. There are two main reasons for this:

1   Egypt was much more developed agriculturally and industrially than its neighbours when it embarked upon the Aswan High Dam project
2   Sudan and Ethiopia have spent the last two decades involved with civil wars.

The Nile in Egypt is a river with an annual flood life-cycle upon which the traditional farming practices were based. The monthly discharge at Aswan used to vary from 700 cumecs in May, to over 8000 cumecs in September at the height of the flood

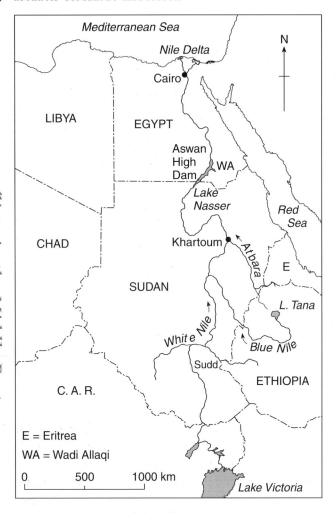

Figure 3.5 *The course of the Nile*

Figure 3.6 *The Nile at Aswan*

season. When the Aswan High Dam began operating in 1971, the flow pattern was evened out; the creation of Lake Nasser, with a normal storage capacity of 108 billion m³, enabled the Egyptians to regulate how much water flowed into the Nile. Egypt's agriculture was transformed by the building of the dam, particularly in the north where perennial irrigation replaced seasonal irrigation. Within 15 years, the area under crops was almost tripled and double-cropping (two harvests a year) became commonplace.

Many negative ecological side effects have resulted from the building of the Aswan High Dam, due to the new water levels, the deposition of silt in Lake Nasser close to the dam, the increased use of chemical fertilisers and the spread of diseases such as bilharzia. (See Figure 3.7).

Despite the initial success of the Aswan Dam, it does not appear to have solved the problems of drought and flood. In the mid to late 1980s, drought in Ethiopia led to very low levels in the Nile and in Egypt water levels were 20 to 50 per cent below

average, which had an impact on irrigation capacity, navigability of the river and electricity supplies. As a result of this, Egypt had to revise its policy relating to how much water could be released each month from Lake Nasser, which already loses 10 per cent of its capacity each year through evaporation.

Egypt's population growth is outstripping any increases in crop production, so the country relies heavily upon food imports, and new areas away from the Nile valley are being examined for their irrigation potential. One such location is the Wadi Allaqi, the main eastern tributary into Lake Nasser. Here aquifers, partly fed by seepage from the lake are used as a source of irrigation for a pilot scheme agricultural settlement of 200 people – many similar villages are planned for the future.

In the 1960s Ethiopia and the Sudan had small populations in comparison with Egypt; now the situation is changing. At present, Ethiopia has around 58 million people, but by 2025, at current growth rates, this is likely to become 117 million, as opposed to 97 million in Egypt. Sudan's population will probably grow to around 45 million by 2025.

The bigger threat to Egypt is likely to come from Ethiopia, a non-Arab country with no signed water agreements. After decades of internal turmoil, Ethiopia has been at peace since 1992, and is now involved in rebuilding its economy. Known as 'the water tower of Africa', it is the source of 11 rivers which ultimately feed into the Nile – contributing 80 per cent of the water which eventually flows through Egypt. Heavy erosion from the deforested hillsides puts an estimated 2000 tonnes of soil per square kilometre per year into Ethiopia's rivers; large-scale hydro-engineering schemes would help to stabilise the watersheds in the region. In the 1960s and 1970s US advisers identified 26 places where hydroelectric dams and reservoirs could be

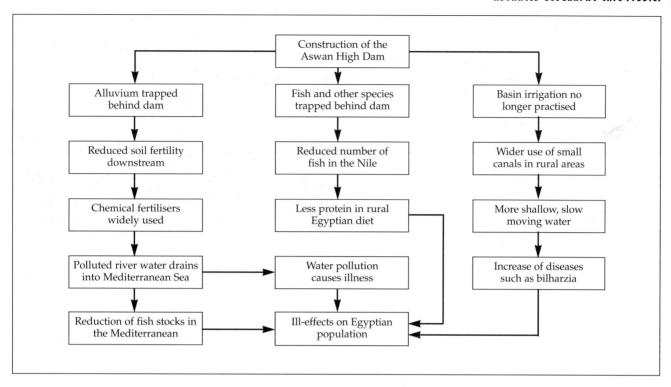

Figure 3.7 *The environmental effects of the Aswan Dam*

established in the Ethiopian Highlands and Ethiopia itself has proposed some 40 new irrigation schemes. Once the country starts using its water resources more fully, there will be severe problems of water supply downstream in Egypt.

THE TIGRIS AND EUPHRATES BASINS

The two rivers which gave birth to the ancient civilisations of Mesopotamia rise in the mountains of Eastern Anatolia in Turkey: the Euphrates flows through Syria into Iraq and the Tigris straight from Turkey into Iraq – they join to become the Shatt-al-Arab before flowing into the Gulf (see Figure 3.8). The changing use of these waters by these unfriendly neighbours has led to great tension in the region.

Until the 1970s, there were no large-scale dams on the Tigris or Euphrates – just barrages for small-scale local irrigation projects; and therefore few water-supply problems were experienced in downstream Iraq. Between 1968 and 1975 Syria's Tabqa Dam was constructed, ponding up 40 000 million m³ of water in Lake Assad. This added 600 000 hectares to the country's farmland, creating a new agricultural region close to the Turkish border. The project was carried out with Iraqi agreement.

In the early 1970s, Turkey embarked upon its South East Anatolian development project (GAP), which involved 12 separate schemes on the Tigris

and Euphrates. Overall, the project will irrigate 1.6 million hectares of land and increase Turkey's electricity capacity by 70 per cent, thereby transforming the country's poorest region. Various smaller dams were inaugerated in the 1970s and 1980s (e.g. the Keban Dam), but the largest, the Atatürk Dam was opened in 1995.

No agreement had to be made between Syria and Turkey, because Turkey financed the scheme itself; by contrast, when countries borrow money from the IMF for such projects, they are obliged to make arrangements with their neighbours. The Atatürk Dam, named after the founder of modern Turkey, is regarded as a prestige engineering achievement of great national pride to the Turks; to environmentalists it is yet another 'mega-dam' which will create yet more ecological problems. The Keban Dam is already silting up much faster than envisaged, but this is hardly surprising, given the rapid rates of gulley erosion on the hillsides of semi-arid Eastern Anatolia.

The Euphrates' discharge over the border into Syria was orignally 30 billion m³ per annum, but when the GAP is fully operational, this total could be reduced by as much as 60 per cent. Already, the level of Lake Assad has dropped significantly and Syrian villagers are finding the quality of irrigation water much poorer, which is affecting both their crop yields and their health. Under pressure, Turkey eventually agreed to release an extra 500 cumecs of

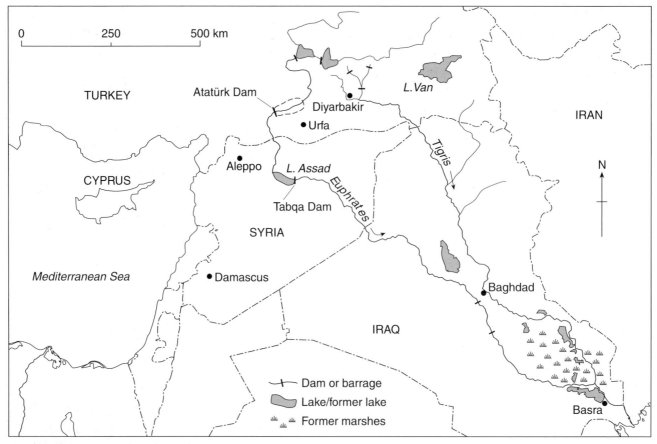

Figure 3.8 *The Tigris and Euphrates basins*

Figure 3.9 *Fishermen in the Euphrates, S. Iraq*

water through the Euphrates, although this was a trade-off with the Syrians to stop them from harbouring the Kurdish PKK guerillas, who are fighting for independence from Turkey.

Much further downstream in Iraq, up to 90 per cent of the water flow from the Euphrates is likely to be lost. Already, over-irrigation and poor water quality around Basra in Southern Iraq have led to high salinity levels in soils; when the GAP scheme is completely operational in the year 2005, the situation is likely to be far worse.

Figure 3.10 *A dam in Syria*

THE JORDAN BASIN

The water situation along the Eastern Mediterranean coastlands is made extremely complicated by the political situation. Although better watered than many parts of the Middle East (over 1000 mm per annum on the Lebanon Ranges and 600–800 mm per annum on the hills of Galilee and Judea), there is a much denser population to support.

The River Jordan, the largest surface water resource in the area, has been described as a 'muddy, brackish, unimpressive river'; its average discharge at the King Hussein Bridge is a mere 32.5 cumecs (compared with 2650 cumecs on the Nile at Aswan). The Jordan is fed by streams from the highlands surrounding its headwaters and some larger tributary rivers such as the Yarmuk.

The main conflict in the region is between Israel and its Arab neighbours, particularly Jordan, and within the current confines of Israel, between Jews and Palestinians. Following the foundation of the state of Israel in 1948 and the consequent heavy immigration, the comprehensive development of water resources was a top priority; new supplies were needed to support rapid urban growth and to increase agricultural output, especially in the more arid south where irrigation was taken to the Negev Desert.

In 1951 Lake Hula and its surrounding marshes was drained and Israel started to build its National Water Carrier to take water from the north and distribute it southwards, (see Figure 3.11). This has brought Israel into dispute with Jordan, which relies on the resources of the same river (but further downstream), and was one of the reasons for the 1967 Six Days War between Israel and its neighbours. One of the consequences of the war was Israel's occupation of the Syrian Golan Heights, which secured more of the River Jordan's headwater supplies for Israel, and the Palestinian West Bank from which Israel already extracted groundwater.

Jordan responded to Israel's National Water Carrier by constructing a parallel project, the East Ghor Canal; this has, however, put Jordan in conflict with Syria over the use of the waters of the River Yarmuk and its tributaries.

Currently, Israel takes 570 million m³ of water per year from the River Jordan, but 850 million m³ come from groundwater sources. The aquifers along the coastal belt are being over-exploited and there is considerable seawater seepage into the

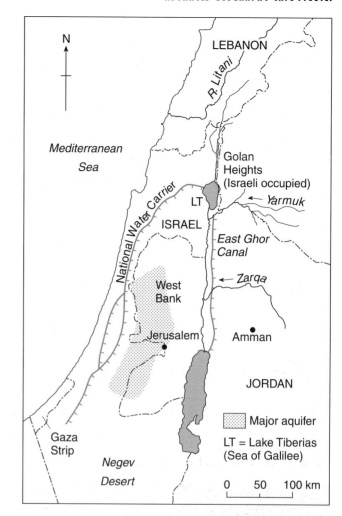

Figure 3.11 *Countries of the Jordan basin*

water table. Further inland are much more abundant groundwater resources, under the hills of Samaria and Judea in the West Bank; it is estimated that Israel consumes 80 per cent of the water extracted from these aquifers. This is not surprising when average consumption figures are compared: Israelis use 300 litres per person per day on a par with Europeans, whereas Palestinians and Jordanians use only 80 litres per person per day. As the Israelis increase their settlements and farms on Palestinian territory the situation will deteriorate. The Palestinian *intifada* or civil disobedience uprising has its roots partly in the Israeli handling of the water issue.

MAN AND SUPERPLAN

Both Saddam Hussein in Iraq and Colonel Gaddafi in Libya have taken great personal interest in large-scale schemes to build canals through the desert.

water resource conflicts in the Middle East

In December 1992, a year after the Second Gulf War, Iraq inaugurated its 'Third River' or 'Saddam River', a 565 km canal which cuts through the marshlands of Southern Iraq between Baghdad and Basra (see Figure 3.12). Although the waterway is, theoretically, designed to carry clean irrigation water to an area of high soil salinity, (summer temperatures can soar to 40 °C in this region), there appear to be ulterior motives for its construction.

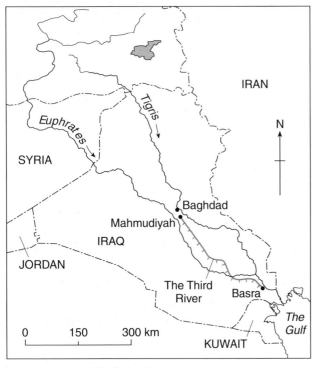

Figure 3.12 *The 'Third River'*

The marshes are the traditional home of the *Ma'dan* or Marsh Arabs, whose culture and lifestyle go back some 5000 years. These marsh dwellers are independently minded Shi'ite Moslems who oppose Saddam Hussein's regime. Some of their territory was badly damaged in the 1991 war, but the draining of the land as a result of the waterway's construction will displace some 50 000 *Ma'dan* in the Al Amarah, Al Hammar and Al Hawizah marshes. The traditional culture of people living in fine reed-built houses (*mudhifs*) and travelling by long wooden boats (*mushufs*), is being destroyed; likewise the wildlife species unique to the marshes, such as the otter, ibis and wild pig, are also doomed to extinction.

In Lybia, Colonel Gaddafi started his 'Great Man-Made River' project in 1984. Its purpose is to carry water from the Kufra and Sarir sandstone aquifers in the south to the more populated areas along the Mediterranean coast, especially the two major cities of Tripoli and Bengazi (see Figure 3.13). The canal network will be 4200 km long and 140 wells have been drilled or planned. Each year, 2.2 billion m³ of

water will be transported, the journey from south to north taking nine days during which there will be considerable loss through evaporation. Sarir was planned to be the centre of a great agriculturally productive oasis to be worked by immigrants from the north, but the plan fell through. Estimates suggest that the Sarir water table is declining at a rate of 2 m per year.

Along the Mediterranean where the main source of water is local aquifers, population growth and water demands have led to a lowering of the water table and sea water contamination (now a familiar problem in the Middle East).

The deep aquifers of the Lybian desert hold part of the estimated 60 000 km³ of water held in storage under the entire Sahara. This is fossil water left over from a more pluvial period when Northern Europe was covered in ice sheets and the Sahara was rich grassland. Once used, fossil water cannot be replaced; this is especially worrying to the Egyptians as the aquifers stretch over the border into their territory. Even more serious, Libya's water abstraction could already be affecting the level of the Nile, by increasing its rate of seepage into sandstone strata. Egyptian geologists are also studying their aquifers in the Western Desert for future large-scale expansion of agriculture in such places as the Siwa Oasis. Libya and Egypt briefly went to war in 1977; they are not the friendliest of neighbours and water demands could set off future conflicts between them.

A newspaper article of December 1997 sheds a completely different light on the purpose of Gaddafi's 'Great Man-Made River' (see Figure 3.14).

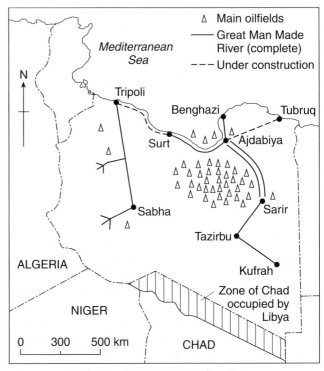

Figure 3.13 *Libya's 'Great Man-Made River'*

Mystery of Gadafy's warren

IN THE expanse of Libya's desert, where temperatures climb towards 40C on a winter's day, an army of more than 12,000 foreign workers is toiling on one of the world's most ambitious and mysterious public works projects.

Drilling rigs rise 60 feet in the air, their gigantic hammers and powerful drilling bits boring more than a quarter of a mile into the earth. Hundreds of trucks haul sections of concrete pipe, 13 feet in diameter, which are lowered into place by huge cranes and buried beneath the sand.

Libya calls it the Great Man-Made River project, and says the pipes, wells and pumping stations will one day make the desert bloom from Tripoli to Kufra.

But three engineers working on the £15 billion project, interviewed seperately, suspect that it has a clandestine military purpose.

"If Saddam Hussein said he was building a four metre (13ft) pipe to 100 miles from Kuwait, 100 miles from Iran, 100 miles from Turkey, for the purpose of moving water, would you believe him?" asked one European engineer.

Such a tunnel could accommodate military vehicles or even a railway.

When it is completed, Libya will have more than 2,000 miles of tunnel stretching from Tunisia to Egypt. In the south, it will reach almost to Sudan and Chad – a country with which Libya has tense relations.

Huge underground storage areas are being built at intervals along the pipes. The engineers say they are more elaborate than would be needed for holding water. Made of reinforced concrete, they would be suitable for holding

troops or military supplies, including chemical weapons. They would let Muammar Gadafy, the Libyan leader, conceal his activities from the American spy satellites that pass over each day.

"This is the first real evidence of something which has been suspected for several years," said Paul Beaver, a defence and intelligence analyst with Jane's Defence Weekly.

"Gadafy seems to have taken a leaf out of [the late North Korean dictator] Kim Il-sung's book and created a potential military arsenal underground."

Figure 3.14 *Article from* **The Guardian** *Thursday December 4 1997*

SUMMARY

- 80 per cent of Middle East is arid
- Wettest places on the region's fringes
- Very high summer temperature, evapotranspiration and water deficiency rates
- Six main sources of water
- Major rivers (Nile, Tigris, Euphrates) and deep aquifers cross borders
- Nile = 10 per cent of Africa's area; two main sources
- Potential conflict with Ethiopia in future (source of 80 per cent of Nile)
- Environmental changes caused by Aswan Dam
- 1980s drought severely lowered water levels

- Euphrates crosses Turkey, Syria and Iraq
- 1975 Tabqa Dam (Syria); 1995 Atatürk Dam (Turkey)
- 60 per cent reduction of water in Syria, 90 per cent in Iraq
- Jordan basin conflicts: Israel *v* Jordan, Israel *v* Palestinians, Syria *v* Jordan
- National Water Carrier (Israel); East Ghor Canal (Jordan)
- 565 km Saddam River destroying Marsh Arab culture
- Libya's 'Great Man-Made River', 4200 km project,

EXAMINATION QUESTIONS

This case study, although directly involving water supply, could also be used in relation to natural resources in general, and in relation to questions which involve competition for resources between countries. There are several 'case studies within the case study' enabling any combination of examples from the Middle East to be used, on their own or with examples from other parts of the world.

SPECIFIC

Examples of specific questions using the case study:

1. With reference to places you have studied, examine the contention that water is the world's most valuable economic resource.
2. 'Water is an unevenly distributed resource, not always available where most needed.' Examine this statement and suggest, with actual examples you have studied, how water supply problems may be solved.

GENERAL

Wider use of materials can be applied in relation to questions on natural resources and possible conflicts between countries:

3. 'The world's wealth is unevenly distributed because of the uneven distribution of natural resources.' Critically examine this statement.
4. 'In an increasingly interdependent world, the sharing of technology and resources is becoming increasingly important.' Examine this statement in relation to countries you have studied.

— CASE STUDY — 4
THE CLIMATIC BELTS AND ENVIRONMENTS OF AFRICA

> *... Africa often is misunderstood. There are numerous generalisations, yet few are valid when examined within the diverse realities of the continent. This situation often arises because of a single specific case has been extrapolated to represent the whole of the continent ...*
>
> Lewis and Berry, *African Environments and Resources*

There is little doubt about the truth of the statement, above; in comparison with other continents, Africa is too often regarded as a homogeneous land mass with a problem climate, a degraded environment and a population suffering from disease and malnutrition. Some of this misunderstanding is due to the continent's mainly tropical location, but mostly derives from the way in which the media have given simplistic coverage to problems such as drought in the Sahel and famine in Ethiopia.

GEOGRAPHICAL LOCATION, SHAPE AND RELIEF

Africa, with an area of 30 216 000 km² (roughly three times that of Europe), is the second largest continent; it therefore accounts for approximately 20 per cent of the Earth's land mass. As the most tropical of all continents, it has the highest overall average temperatures throughout the year. However, within the continent, there are huge variations in climate which give rise to five major biomes and a great variety of more localised ecosystems. The latitudinal position of Africa is what determines the broad patterns of climatic and vegetation zones, yet the shape of the continent and its pattern of relief are what determines the considerable regional variations in temperature and rainfall distribution.

Figure 4.1 shows the latitudinal position of Africa. Three important factors arise from this:

1   Africa extends almost exactly the same distance north and south of the equator, giving it a 'mirror image' pattern of climate on either side of latitude 0°.

2   With over 75 per cent of its area between the tropics of Capricorn and Cancer, it is almost entirely influenced by tropical weather systems; mid-latitude westerly winds and depressions touch only the continent's northern and southern extremities.

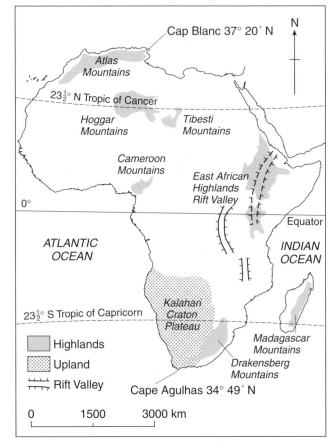

Figure 4.1 *The latitudinal location of Africa; Relief features which influence Africa's climate*

3   A large proportion of the continent is influenced by the sub-tropical high pressure belts, located between 20° and 30° N and S (shifting seasonally), making aridity a major feature of the African climate.

The shape of Africa is far from symmetrical. Much more of the continent lies to the north of the equator than to the south. It also lacks a proper ocean boundary in the north-east where the Red Sea adjoins the Arabian Peninsula. This explains why the desert areas are so much broader in Northern Africa than in Southern

Africa. This has a significant impact upon the annual average rainfall totals throughout the continent, which show great asymmetry between north and south.

Latitudinal belt	Annual average rainfall
40°–30° N	220 mm
30°–20° N	37 mm
20°–10° N	550 mm
10°–0° N	1380 mm
0°–10° S	1320 mm
10°–20° S	1070 mm
20°–30° S	570 mm
30°–40° S	509 mm

Geologically, a large part of Africa is made up of ancient eroded plateaux. High elevations moderate what would otherwise be considerably higher temperatures in a lot of Southern and Central Africa (e.g. over 90 per cent of the land of Zimbabwe and Botswana is above 1000 m). The highest mountain ranges (the Atlas, the Ethiopian and East African Highlands, and the Drakensberg) all have strong regional influences on temperatures and rainfall; yet Africa lacks a major continuous mountain chain, such as the Andes in South America and the Rockies in North America, capable of influencing the climate of the entire continent. (Figure 4.1 also shows the main relief features of Africa).

AFRICA AND THE ITCZ

As Africa is so tropical, its climates are bound up with the annual movement of the ITCZ (Intertropical Convergence Zone), which is part of the pattern of global atmospheric circulation. The predominent pattern of air movement across the surface of Africa involves the trade winds, blowing from the north-east and south-east converging at the low pressure belt located on, or close to, the equator. From here the air rises, moves polewards and sinks back to the surface to create the subtropical high pressure belts associated with the desert areas.

The ITCZ shifts because of the seasonal migration of the intense heat generated by the vertical midday sun between the two Tropics. In the northern summer the ITCZ lies across the Sahara, whereas in the northern winter the ITCZ lies much further south – although the configuration of land and sea bends it into a reverse 'S' shape (see Figure 4.2).

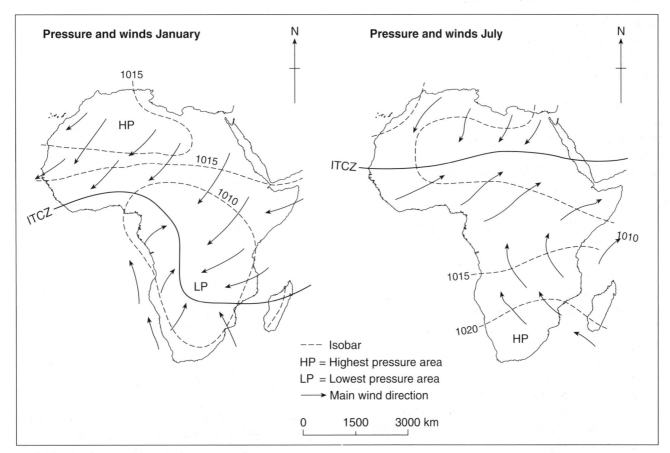

Figure 4.2 *The changing position of the ITCZ*

The annual movement of the ITCZ is the most important factor in determining when each part of Africa will get its rainy season. The high-rainfall equatorial belt which straddles Central Africa tends to have two rainfall maxima, in the spring and the autumn, when the ITCZ is over the equator. By contrast, the savanna regions have just one rainy season which occurs from June to August in the Northern Hemisphere and from November to January in the Southern Hemisphere, again coinciding with the presence of the ITCZ. (Figure 4.3 shows the rainfall season pattern for the whole continent).

RAINFALL AND EVAPOTRANSPIRATION

Although the rainfall pattern of Africa is dominated by latitude and the seasonal position of the ITCZ, there are other more localised factors which need to be taken into account when explaining the annual rainfall totals (see Figure 4.3).

The most extensive area of high rainfall stretches across the equatorial belt of Africa, along the Guinea Coast and through the Congo/Zäire Basin, whereas the most extensive dry areas coincide with the high pressure belts of the Sahara and Namib–Kalahari deserts. The savanna lands of the continent are essentially transition zones between these two

extremes and consequently have a moderate rainfall. The northern and southern tips of Africa also have the moderate level of rainfall associated with their Mediterranean-type climates.

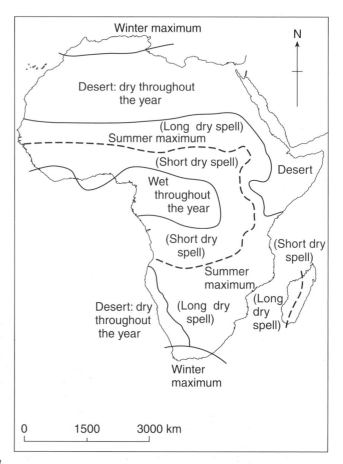

Figure 4.4 *A baobab grove in Mali*

Relief has a marked effect upon rainfall patterns. In the north, the areas of the highest rainfall are in the more elevated parts of the Atlas Mountains in Morocco and Algeria. The Ethiopian Highlands, with numerous peaks over 3500 m, provide Africa with its largest zone of relief-generated rainfall. In southern Africa, the Drakensberg are responsible for localised areas of high

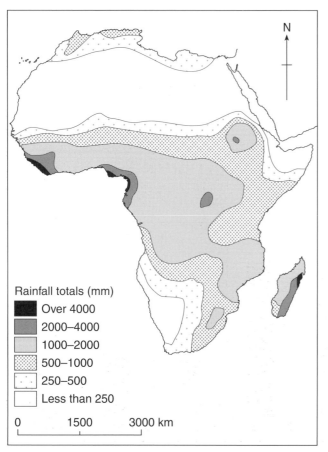

Figure 4.3a *Annual rainfall totals;* **b** *Seasonal pattern of rainfall*

rainfall, such as in the mountain kingdom of Lesotho. Madagascar is the part of Africa most influenced by onshore trade winds which bring high orographic rainfall to the island. Some parts of the eastern, mountainous side of the island receive over 3000 mm of rain per year, whereas in the rain shadow of the western side of the island, rainfall is, in places, as low as 500 mm. A similar high rainfall from the South East Trades is experienced along the coast of Mozambique. Although Africa does not suffer from tropical cyclones as much as South East Asia or the Caribbean, conditions for their formation are ideal in that part of the Indian Ocean off the south-eastern coast; consequently, Madagascar and Mozambique are the two countries most affected by storm damage, although the cyclones occasionally hit Swaziland and the South African province of KwaZulu/Natal. Ten to twelve cyclones reach Africa each year, contributing considerably to the rainfall totals of the south-east.

There are three rainfall anomaly areas within Africa where annual totals are much lower than their latitudes would dictate.

1   **The Horn of Africa** (Somalia and Eastern Ethiopia), is arid and much of Kenya is semi-arid. The reasons for this are not fully understood, but the way in which heavy rainfall in eastern Madagascar creates a rain shadow effect in the lee of the South East Trade winds and the configuration of the coast parallel to the North East Trades may explain why neither of these prevailing winds brings much seasonal rain to East Africa.

2   **The Guinea Coast**. Along the high rainfall region of the West African coast, there is a much drier area in Eastern Ghana, Togo and Benin, known as the Dahomey Gap. The trend of the coastline and the upwelling of cold waters offshore are both possible contributing factors.

3   **The coast of Angola**. The influence of the arid zone of the Skeleton Coast of Namibia stretches a long way north into Angola. This can be explained by the presence of the cold Benguela Current which is partly responsible for the existence of the Namib Desert, as it creates coastal and offshore fogs and prevents potential rainfall moisture from penetrating further inland.

Evapotranspiration rates are high in Africa because of the large amounts of incoming solar radiation; the actual evapotranspiration (AE) pattern which reflects the availability of water is at its lowest in the Sahara (30 mm) and its highest in the equatorial zone (just under 1000 mm). By contrast, the rates for potential evapotranspiration (PE) are much higher throughout

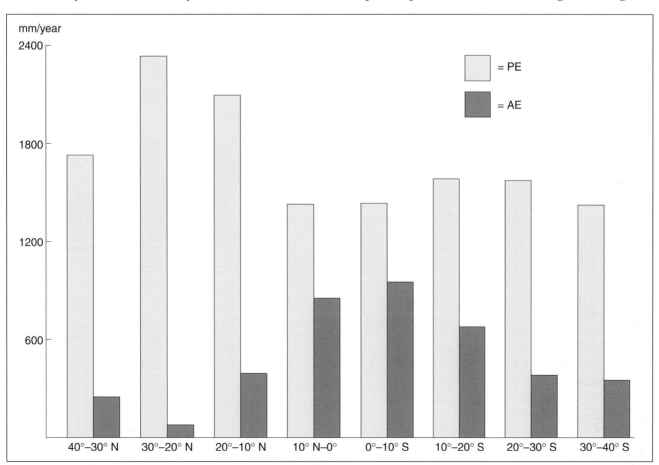

Figure 4.5 *Actual and potential evapotranspiration rates by latitude*

Africa, but in the opposite order. Values of over 2500 mm are common under the cloudless skies of the Sahara and Namib deserts, whereas the much lower rates of around 1400 mm are typical under humid, cloudy skies of Equatorial Africa (see Figure 4.5).

TEMPERATURE RANGES

As a mainly tropical continent, Africa is not too affected by extreme temperature ranges. The main determinants of the differences between the highest and lowest temperatures for individual locations are latitude, cloud cover and, to a lesser extent, latitude. The highest temperature ranges are found in the desert

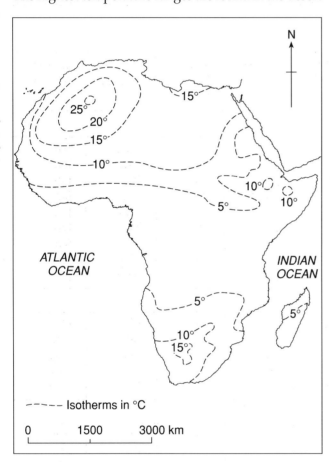

Figure 4.6 *Temperature range*

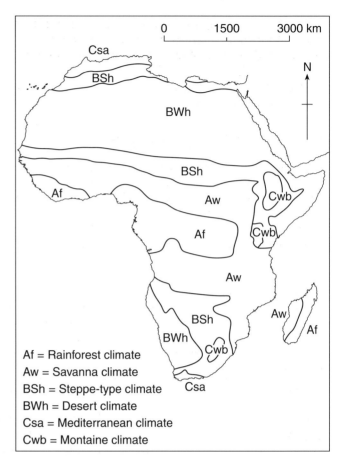

Af = Rainforest climate
Aw = Savanna climate
BSh = Steppe-type climate
BWh = Desert climate
Csa = Mediterranean climate
Cwb = Montaine climate

Figure 4.7 *Köppen's climate classification*

Figure 4.8 *Location of African climate stations*

areas just outside the Tropics, where the higher latitude causes greater seasonal changes in the angle of incoming solar rays and high pressure gives rise to clear skies for much of the year. High diurnal temperature ranges are also experienced in these desert areas, especially in the winter months and in mountain areas (e.g. the Tibesti and Hoggar ranges in the Sahara).

The main region to have a high temperature range because of its elevation is the Ethiopian Highlands.

Equatorial Africa, by contrast, has much lower temperature ranges which are accounted for by the constantly high angle of the sun's rays throughout the year and the high degree of cloud cover.

Figure 4.6 shows the pattern of temperature ranges for the African continent.

CLIMATIC CLASSIFICATION AND CLIMATE STATIONS

Any classification of the climates of Africa will be dominated by the moisture factor. Köppen's classification (Figure 4.7), shows clearly how climate zones are closely related to the main vegetation zones. Griffiths, in his world survey of climates, recognised 12 distinct climatic zones within Africa; but, as with any classification, it gives sharp boundaries for what are really transition zones. Only where there is a clear break in relief are there sharp boundaries between climate zones (e.g. the differences between the east and west sides of Madagascar and the area around the Drakensberg Mountains).

Figure 4.9 gives statistics for 28 climate stations throughout Africa. The places located in Western and Central Africa are those with the most typically equatorial climates, with high rainfall and a low temperature range; the wettest/driest and hottest/coldest months are largely determined by which side of the equator the towns are located. Accra is the odd place out in terms of rainfall, as it lies within the anomolous dry zone of the Guinea Coast.

Station	Altitude (m)	Total Rainfall (mm)	Wettest Month	Driest Month	Temp. Range (°C)	Hottest Month	Coldest Month
North Africa							
Algiers	50	729	Dec	Jul	18	Aug	Jan
Aswan	194	1	Mar	–	18	Aug	Jan
Cairo	75	25	Dec	Jul	16	Jul	Jan
In Salah	293	14	Dec	J, J, A	28	Aug	Jan
Khartoum	380	179	Aug	N – F	10	May	Jan
Njemena	295	636	Aug	D – F	10	Mar	Dec
Nouachott	5	142	Aug	Jan	10	Sep	Jan
Ouagadougou	306	881	Aug	Jan	10	May	Jan
Tunis	65	444	Jan	Jul	15	Aug	Jan
East Africa							
Addis Ababa	2410	787	Aug	Dec	5	Mar	Dec
Djibouti	7	129	Mar	Jun	12	Jul	Dec
Kampala	1145	1524	Apr	Jan	4	Mar	Aug
Mogadishu	15	399	Jun	Feb	3	Apr	Aug
Nairobi	1616	788	Apr	Jul	5	Mar	Aug
Western and Central Africa							
Accra	60	787	Jun	Jan	3	Mar	Aug
Bangui	380	1574	Aug	Jan	2	Apr	Sep
Kisangani	395	1771	Dec	Jul	1	n/a	n/a
Lagos	40	1464	Jun	Dec	4	Mar	Aug
Libreville	10	2727	Nov	Jul	4	Mar	Aug
Southern Africa							
Antanarivo	1312	1361	Jan	Jul	7	Feb	Jul
Cape Town	44	505	Jun	Jan	10	Dec	Aug
Harare	1480	839	Jan	Jul	8	Oct	Jul
Lusaka	1154	810	Jan	Jul	10	Oct	Jul
Maseru	1528	691	Jan	Jun	14	Jan	Jul
Maputo	60	760	Jan	Jul	7	Mar	Jul
Namibe	44	48	Mar	Jul	10	Mar	Jul
Windhoek	1728	344	Dec	Jul	12	Dec	Jun

Figure 4.9 *Climatic stations of Africa – statistics*

the climatic belts and environments of Africa

All stations of East Africa fall within the drier climate zone found in that part of the continent; however, Kampala's more westerly location gives it a higher rainfall as it is more open to the influences experienced in Central Africa.

North African stations lie within three different zones: the Mediterranean (Tunis and Algiers), the Sahara (Aswan, Cairo, In Salah, Khartoum, Nouachott), and the Sahel dry savanna zone (Njemena, Ouagadougou); their rainfall figures vary accordingly. Temperature ranges reflect both latitude and levels of cloud cover – In Salah, in the centre of the Sahara, has a range of 28 °C, the highest for any station listed.

Southern African stations reflect similar influences to those in the north, but with the seasons reversed. Cape Town has a Mediterranean type climate, whereas Namibe and Windhoek are within the desert zone; the other locations experience the seasonal changes typical of savanna lands, with the exception of Tantanarivo, which receives the localised Madagascar 'monsoon'.

AFRICA'S ECOSYSTEMS

Africa has four of the world's major biomes – the tropical rainforest, the savanna grasslands, deserts and the Mediterranean type vegetation, as well as montane ecosystems in highland areas. Each of these is a direct adaption to the climatic characteristics of the area in which it is found and, although climate is only one of many factors which influence flora and fauna, it is by far the most important. (Figure 4.10 locates Africa's main vegetation regions.)

TROPICAL RAINFORESTS

The tropical lowland or evergreen forest of Africa stretches across the equatorial belt, along the Guinea Coast into the Zaire/Congo Basin, where it covers some 1.8 million km^2. A small outpost of this forest is to be found on the eastern side of the island of Madagascar. These forests, which are extremely rich in biodiversity, are associated with rainfall over 1400 mm per annum, high humidity and continually high temperatures.

The subject of Case Study 6, Africa's rainforest will not be dealt with in further detail here.

THE SAVANNAS

The savannas occupy 65 per cent of the land mass of Africa, where they surround the rainforest zone like a great horseshoe. Savanna, although also known as tropical grassland, is diverse in character, varying according to rainfall, and is essentially a transition zone between forest and desert.

It is the length of the dry season (which may vary from a few weeks to nine months), rather than the annual rainfall total, which is the main climatic determinant of the particular vegetation structure of the savanna region. From semi-deciduous forest in the wettest parts, savanna develops into more open parkland scattered with microphyllous trees as the dry season lengthens; where the climate is drier still, the parkland gives way to grassland with the occasional tree, then to more stunted grasses and bushes and eventually to scrubland on the desert fringes. Typical savanna tree species include the acacia with its umbrella shape and microphyllous leaves for low rates of transpiration, and the *adamsonia digitara* or baobab, which stores moisture in its fleshy trunk.

It is believed that the savannas, unlike the rainforests, are a relatively new biome, which have evolved as a result of climate changes during the last few million years.

THE DESERTS

In Africa, the true deserts are dry and, generally, the

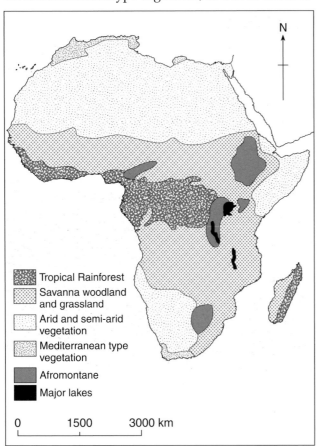

Figure 4.10 *Main vegetation zones of Africa*

N

Tropical Rainforest
Savanna woodland and grassland
Arid and semi-arid vegetation
Mediterranean type vegetation
Afromontane
Major lakes

0   1500   3000 km

100 mm annual isohyet is taken as its upper limit boundary between arid and semi-arid zones, rather than the more usual 250 mm per annum. Unlike the savanna, there is no direct connection between areas north and south of the equator, so the Sahara and the Namib/Kalahari have different ranges of species. North African arid and semi-arid areas have over 3000 plant species which adapt themselves to the dry conditions in a variety of ways and include phraetophytes in wadi bottoms, halophytes near salt lakes, ephemerals and succulents. The Namib has a range of plants unlike those found anywhere else in the arid world, including aloes such as the quiver tree (*aloe dichotoma*) and the welwitschia (*welwitschia mirabilis*), a ground-hugging succulent that takes its moisture from coastal fog, and is said to live for over a thousand years.

MEDITERRANEAN AREAS

These are even more widely separated from each other than the deserts, and have evolved as disperate ecosystems. The North African plant formation is similar to that of southern Europe and the Levant, with the full range of communities from sclerophyllous evergreen forests to the secondary maquis in drier places (although euphorbias are more common than in Europe). In the Cape area of South Africa, the typical *finbos* vegetation (a scrub community with many varieties of sclerophyllous plants), as there is a lack of taller plants, fills 'a vacant tree niche'. The zone is also much richer in species than the north with over 8500 plant types within 90 000 km², and a high degree of endemism (68 per cent).

MONTANE AREAS

Each of the mountain areas of Africa has its own range of distinctive species which have evolved in isolation from one another. There is 75 per cent endemism within these communities. As in other mountainous regions of the world, African highlands have different vegetation zones according to altitude and, therefore, climate.

The most striking plants of the Afromontane biome are those of the high-altitude communities in East Africa where, on the equatorial mountains between 2500 and 3000 m, there is a zone of giant ericaceous plants such as the lobelia. These plants are believed to have evolved here as a result of the high incidence of ultra-violet rays at this altitude.

CLIMATIC CHANGE

Much has been written about present desertification in Africa but, throughout the continent, there is evidence of climatic change on a variety of scales, over geological time, prehistoric time and historic time. Figure 4.11 includes some the evidence for climate change.

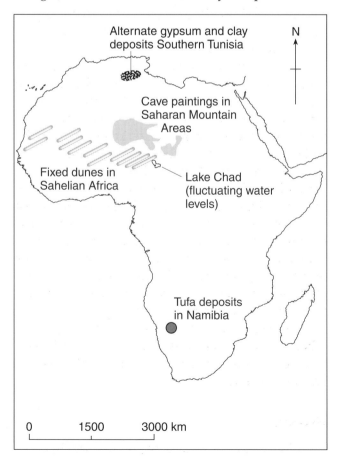

Figure 4.11 *Evidence of climatic change*

Figure 4.12 *The "Grand Erg Oriental" in the Tunisian Sahara*

Figure 4.13 *Zebras at a waterhole during the dry season in Namibia*

Five of the most important ways of identifying the changes are:

1 The existence of 'fossil dunes' throughout the dry savanna, in places such as near the Bandigiara Escarpment in Mali, suggest that the climate in the past was much drier.

2 Changing lake levels. Lake Chad was at least five times its present size during the Pleistocene period. Its levels have fluctuated ever since, rather than simply declining.

3 Large tufa deposits, like petrified waterfalls in the Naukluft Mountains of Namibia suggest much wetter climatic periods in the past.

4 Around the Chott-et-Djerid and other salt lakes in North Africa, interbedded clay and gypsum deposits relate to the alternate wet and dry periods of the past.

5 Throughout the Sahara, archaeological remains and cave paintings suggest that much larger populations of human and animals inhabited the area in the prehistoric past – 8000 to 9000 years ago.

SUMMARY

- 20 per cent of Earth's land mass
- Most tropical of all the continents
- Symmetrical latitudinally
- Importance of the ITCZ
- Relationship between climate and vegetation zones
- Influence of ITCZ and relief on rainfall pattern
- Three rainfall anomaly areas
- Strong differences between AE and PE throughout Africa
- Evidence for climate change throughout Africa

 EXAMINATION QUESTIONS

This case study deals with a broad area. The information can be used for climatological questions as well as ecosystems questions.

SPECIFIC

Examples of questions using the material directly:

1 With reference to an example you have studied, outline the factors which influence climatic patterns at a continental scale.

2 With reference to countries or areas you have studied, how would you attempt to subdivide them into distinct climatic regions?

GENERAL

More general application of the case study could be:

3 With reference to specific examples, explain how vegetation is determined by climatic factors.

4 What evidence may there be for climatic change? Illustrate your answer with specific examples from different parts of the world.

— CASE STUDY — ⑤
THE REGIONAL CLIMATES OF SPAIN

> **Geography's chief subject matter is the control of climates by landscapes, and of landscapes by climates, and the control by both of the environments of living things.**
>
> *Sir Halford Mackinder*

Although the Mediterranean climate is generally summarised by the simple statement 'hot dry summers, warm wet winters', there are many regional abnormalities within the Mediterranean Basin. The popular notion of 'Sunny Spain' belies a country which has enormous regional variations in both temperatures and rainfall. Above all else, two aspects of Spanish geography are responsible for its climatic diversity:

1 It is mountainous, having the second highest average elevation of any country in Europe, after Switzerland.
2 The Iberian Peninsula is a large, square landmass (596 800 km²), which creates a strongly continental climatic effect within Spain.

GEOGRAPHICAL LOCATION AND RELIEF

Spain occupies 80 per cent of the land of the Iberian Peninsula. Of its 17 *Comunidades Autónomas* (autonomous regions), 15 are part of mainland Spain, the other two are island groups: the Balearics in the Mediterranean and the Canaries, which lie 1100 km to the south-west, off the coast of the Western Sahara. The Canary Islands, therefore, have a climate more closely related to that of neighbouring Africa than to Spain. Mainland Spain stretches for almost 6° of latitude and therefore there are considerable differences in temperature between the north of the country and the south.

Spain is influenced by the same five air masses that affect Britain and other parts of Western Europe (see Figure 5.1). In summer, it is in an extension of the Azores high pressure belt that normally imposes the hot, dry anticyclonic regime over the majority of the country for three to four months. In winter, Spain is more of a battleground between anticyclone air from the north and moist, warmer air from the lower pressure areas over the Mediterranean. Each month throughout the winter, an average of five depressions form in the region and pass over Spain.

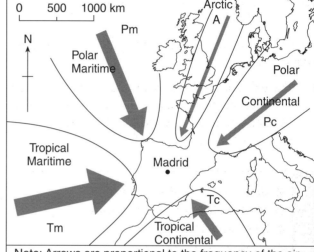

Figure 5.1 *Air masses influencing the Spanish climate*

The relief map of Spain, Figure 5.2, shows how the country is crossed by a series of parallel east–west trending *cordilleras* or mountain chains, which climatically segregate various parts of the land mass. The Pyrenees and the Cantabrian Mountains take the brunt of the cool, moist air coming in from the Atlantic and, consequently, have the highest rainfall in Spain. The Central System of highlands, which includes the Iberian Mountains, cuts the Meseta, Spain's interior tableland plateau, in two and each part has its own distinctive climate. In the south, the Sierra Nevada is the highest range and this has a dramatic rain shadow effect over the south-east coastland, Spain's driest corner.

PATTERNS OF RAINFALL

The rainfall map (Figure 5.4) shows just how close is the relationship between relief and precipitation. The main features to note are:

the regional climates of Spain

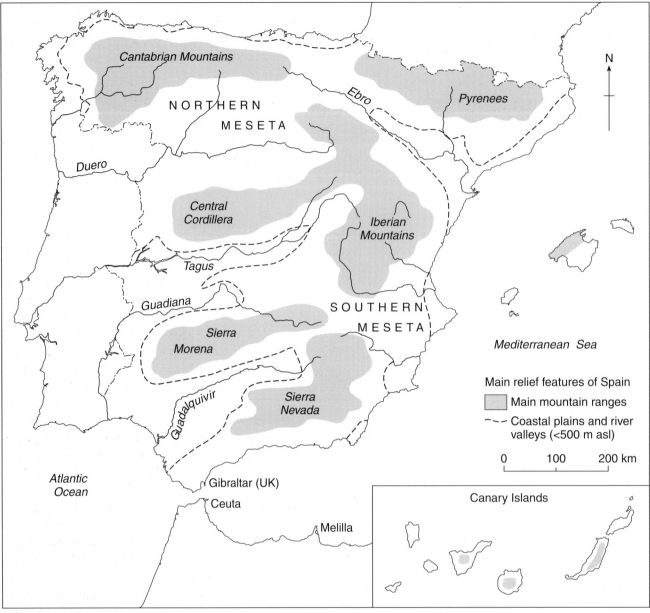

Figure 5.2 *Relief map of Spain*

● The high rainfall of the northern Atlantic coastline and the gradual drop in the rainfall total southwards.

● The general low rainfall of the Meseta, most of which is technically semi-arid (below 500 mm per annum).

● The isolated areas of higher rainfall where the main mountain ranges cut across the peninsula (e.g. Sierra Morena, Central Cordilleras).

● The rain shadow areas with under 300 mm per annum (e.g. the south-east coastlands, the central parts of the Ebro and Duero basins and Southern Mallorca).

● The Canary Islands, apart from their mountain peaks, are also an area of low rainfall, but this is because their main climatic influence is from North Africa.

● In the mountain regions, especially in the north, much of the winter precipitation will be in the form of snowfall rather than rain.

Figure 5.3 *The Cantabrian Mountains near Orviedo*

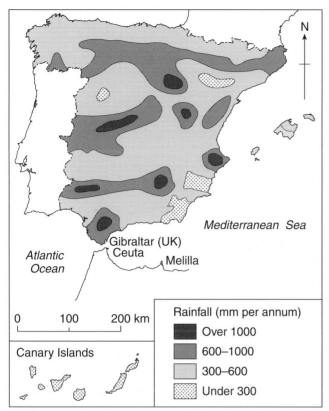

Figure 5.4 *Rainfall in Spain*

CONTINENTALITY

As the patterns of relief have a direct bearing on precipitation, continentality has a similar influence upon temperatures. Spain's climate is moderated by both the Atlantic and the Mediterranean; this is most strongly marked in the winter months (see Figure 5.5a), when both coasts experience mild conditions, although the warmer waters of the Mediterranean and the more southerly latitudes create a 4 °C temperature difference between the Costa del Sol and the Costa Verde. The much lower temperatures experienced over the Meseta are at their most extreme over the Central Cordilleras which may have snow-covered peaks for up to five months. This reflects the way in which elevated relief exaggerates the effects of continentality.

In the summer, the pattern is much more complex (see Figure 5.5b). The Atlantic coastline is still a zone with moderate temperatures, but Central and Southern Spain are strongly influenced by warm continental air from the south and, at the same time, there is an intense build-up of heat in the sheltered basins of the Guadalquivir and Ebro.

The continental influence created by the Iberian Peninsula is even more dramatic when considering temperature ranges. The highest temperature ranges of 21 °C are experienced in the South Eastern

Meseta (Ciudad Real), whereas the lowest ranges (other than in the quasi-tropical Canary Islands) are along the Atlantic coast of Galicia (Vigo), where the benefits of the Gulf Stream are clearly felt.

CLIMATE STATIONS OF SPAIN

Figure 5.7 gives climate statistics for 16 different Spanish cities, scattered throughout the peninsula and islands (see Figure 5.5 for a location map).

Bonaigua, Leitareigas, Seo and Soria, all at over 800 m, have mountain climates where high elevations influence temperatures, especially in winter, when sub-zero conditions are common. Similarly, some of the higher locations on the Meseta (Valladolid, Trujillo, Ciudad Real and Madrid – all located at between 564 and 715 m a.s.l.), have low winter temperatures because of their elevated and exposed positions. By contrast, the most moderate winter temperatures are experienced by the coastal stations of the north (Vigo and San Sebastián), the south (Almería and Alicante) and on the islands (Palma de Mallorca and Santa Cruz de Tenerife).

The stations with the highest rainfall are all located in the north, either on the coast (Vigo and San Sebastián), or in the mountains (Leitareigas in the Cantabrians and Bonaigua in the Pyrenees). The places with the lowest rainfall are those beyond the influence of the Atlantic and which have special local topographical conditions. Almería, with 230 mm of rain per annum is the only location in Europe which is technically true desert, and the local landscapes are characteristically arid. Alicante with 309 mm is in a similar rain shadow situation, and Valladolid with 362 mm is in the sheltered depression of the Duero valley. The proximity of Tenerife to the Sahara accounts for the low rainfall at Santa Cruz.

CLASSIFICATION OF CLIMATES

Various Spanish, British and French geographers have produced different classifications of Spain's regional climates. Figure 5.6 is based on the classification used by Méndez and Molinero in their *Geografía de España*.

The characteristics of each of the regions are:

● **Atlantic zone** (Galicia, Asturias, Cantabria, the Basque provinces and the Pyrenees). A high rainfall total with a winter maximum; moderate winter temperatures at sea level, but sub-zero winter temperatures in the higher mountains. Orographic rainfall from the Atlantic and the

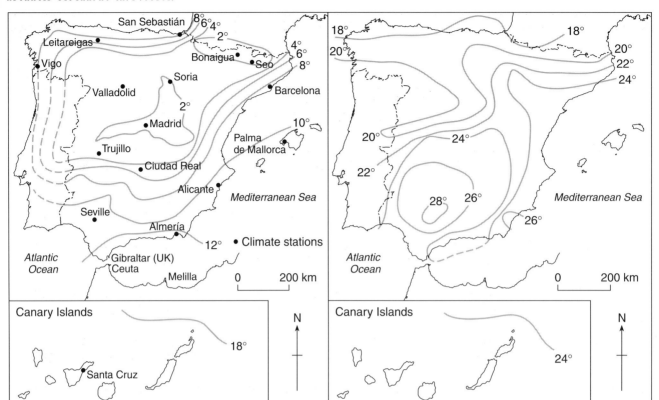

Figure 5.5 *Temperatures and locational climatic stations*

a *Isotherms in January*

b *Isotherms in July*

warm waters of the Gulf Stream are major climatic influences.

● **Northern Meseta** (Castile and Leon). In the rain shadow of the Cantabrian Mountains, therefore low rainfall. The continental effect is strongly felt, resulting in a high temperature range, made more extreme by the altitude of the plateau.

● **Southern Meseta** (Castile–La Mancha, Extremadura). Also a low rainfall region, but with a rain shadow effect caused by the Central Cordilleras. The effects of continentality are more extreme than in the Northern Meseta because of its greater distance from the Atlantic.

● **Ebro Depression** (Aragon). A localised area of very low rainfall because of the rain shadow effect from both the north (Pyrenees) and south (Iberian Mountains). Also very high summer temperatures produced by the basin or 'frying pan' effect.

● **Catalan coast**. Mild winters and hot summers, but localised zone of low rainfall in the rain shadow of the Pyrenees.

● **Valencia coast and Balearics**. The most typically 'Mediterranean' zone in Spain with mild winters, hot summers and moderate rainfall.

● **South-east coast** (Murcia). Mild winters and hot summers, but much drier than any other part of mainland Spain. In the rain shadow of the Sierra

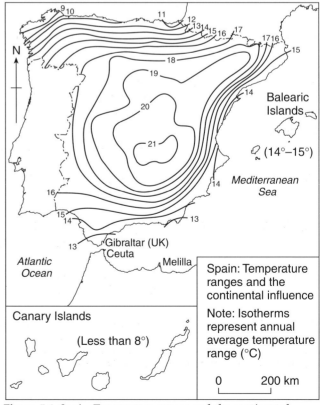

Figure 5.6 *Spain: Temperature ranges and the continental influence*

Station	Altitude (m)		J	F	M	A	M	J	J	A	S	O	N	D	Average temp./ Total rainfall
VIGO	28	Temp. (°C)	10	11	13	14	15	18	20	20	19	16	13	11	15
		Rainfall (mm)	171	135	157	93	101	51	26	43	65	122	187	187	1339
LEITAREIGAS	1525	Temp. (°C)	−2	−2	1	4	5	8	12	10	8	6	2	0	5
		Rainfall (mm)	181	148	177	146	159	103	43	79	138	162	228	202	1739
SAN SEBASTIÁN	258	Temp. (°C)	8	8	11	12	14	17	19	19	18	15	11	8	13
		Rainfall (mm)	135	108	90	102	122	96	95	117	149	161	153	177	1506
BONAIGUA	2263	Temp. (°C)	−3	−2	0	1	5	7	12	12	10	6	2	−1	4
		Rainfall (mm)	76	65	76	104	111	110	77	90	102	139	111	90	1146
SEO DE URGEL	891	Temp. (°C)	3	5	9	12	14	19	21	20	17	12	7	3	12
		Rainfall (mm)	15	31	42	47	81	81	49	83	59	54	37	54	633
BARCELONA	95	Temp. (°C)	9	10	13	14	17	22	24	25	22	18	13	11	17
		Rainfall (mm)	33	42	46	47	52	43	29	48	77	80	49	77	594
VALLADOLID	715	Temp. (°C)	4	5	9	11	14	19	21	21	18	13	8	4	12
		Rainfall (mm)	30	26	42	30	35	33	13	13	28	34	40	40	362
SORIA	1005	Temp. (°C)	1	3	6	8	12	16	19	19	16	11	5	3	10
		Rainfall (mm)	49	48	46	48	57	54	27	26	46	55	47	52	555
MADRID	667	Temp. (°C)	5	7	10	12	17	21	24	23	20	14	10	6	14
		Rainfall (mm)	25	43	37	38	41	37	9	6	36	44	61	43	420
PALMA DE M.	28	Temp. (°C)	10	11	12	15	17	20	24	25	21	17	12	11	17
		Rainfall (mm)	38	33	35	32	27	18	3	10	27	38	26	24	437
TRUJILLO	564	Temp. (°C)	6	8	11	13	17	21	25	25	21	15	9	6	16
		Rainfall (mm)	81	93	81	60	58	26	2	5	40	76	81	73	670
SEVILLE	10	Temp. (°C)	10	12	15	17	20	25	28	28	25	16	15	11	19
		Rainfall (mm)	64	62	93	59	38	9	1	4	22	66	70	84	572
CIUDAD REAL	628	Temp. (°C)	5	7	10	13	16	21	26	25	21	15	9	6	15
		Rainfall (mm)	35	40	52	46	48	23	2	7	23	43	40	45	404
ALICANTE	80	Temp. (°C)	11	12	14	16	19	23	26	26	24	19	15	12	18
		Rainfall (mm)	32	22	18	43	30	14	4	15	47	54	33	30	309
ALMERÍA	7	Temp. (°C)	12	12	14	16	18	22	25	25	23	19	16	13	18
		Rainfall (mm)	31	21	20	28	17	4	0	5	15	26	27	36	230
SANTA CRUZ	37	Temp. (°C)	17	18	18	19	20	22	24	25	24	23	21	18	21
		Rainfall (mm)	36	39	27	13	6	0	0	0	3	31	45	51	252

Figure 5.7 *Climate stations of Spain – statistics*

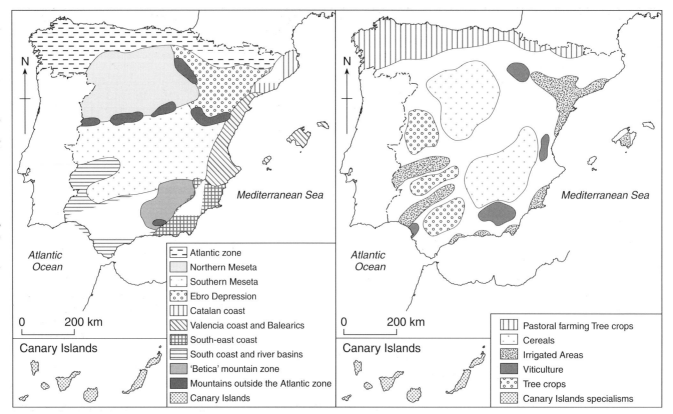

Figure 5.8a *Climatic regions of Spain;* **b** *Agricultural zones of Spain*

Nevada and strongly influenced by airstreams from North Africa.

- **South coast and river basins** (Andalusia, Guadalquivir and Guadiano basins). Low rainfall, warm winters and very hot summers strongly influenced by North Africa; 'frying pan' effect within the river basins. (Seville's temperatures frequently soar to over 40 °C during the summer months.)

- **'Betica' mountain zone** (Sierra Nevada). These are the highest peaks in mainland Spain (rising to 3483 m) which have their own local climate, with snow cover for 3 to 5 months, a higher rainfall and much lower temperatures than the surrounding areas.

- **Mountains outside the Atlantic zone** (e.g. the Central Cordillera). These mountain ranges throughout the Meseta create conditions similar to those experienced in the mountains of the Atlantic zone.

- **Canary Islands.** Located almost in the Tropics (between 25° and 30° N), their climatic influences are different from those of mainland Spain. Low rainfall throughout the year with a winter maximum; high temperatures throughout the year but with a summer maximum.

NATURAL VEGETATION

Climate has a strong influence on the natural vegetation of Spain and, although over 80 per cent of the country's original vegetation cover has been cleared for agriculture, there are still areas which reveal the striking contrasts between north and south as well as highland and lowland.

Figure 5.9 is a cross-section through Spain from the Atlantic coast to the south and on to the Canary Islands showing the pattern of natural vegetation. The wetter, cooler Atlantic coast was originally covered in deciduous oak (*quercus robur*) forest similar to parts of North West Europe, although in the mountains this gives way to pine forest and some higher altitude deciduous trees such as chestnuts and beeches. The Meseta was once covered in the typical Mediterranean evergreen forest composed of trees with sclerophyllous leaves, adapted to summer drought. As one moves south through Spain, three distinct associations of evergreens can be seen, each adapted to successively drier conditions.

On the Northern Meseta, the holm oak (*quercus ilex*) is dominant, but with some cork oaks (*quercus suber*). To the south of the Central Cordilleras, the situation is reversed with the cork oak dominant; today, this is still widely grown throughout Extremadura as a farmed crop for its bark. In the driest parts of the Meseta

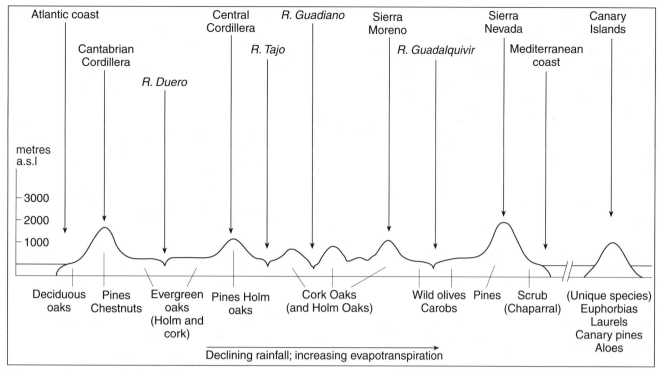

Figure 5.9 *Cross-section through Spain showing natural vegetation*

around the Guadalquivir, evergreen oaks give way to the even more drought-resistant wild olive (*olea sylvestris*) and carob (*ceratonia siliquia*). On the steeper slopes of the coastal ranges which reach down to the Mediterranean, forest gives way to secondary Mediterranean vegetation, scrubland known in Spain as *chaparral*. The Canary Islands have their own unique range of plants, more African than European, which have evolved in isolation to suit the semi-arid climate. Many of the lowland plants are succulents (aloes, euphorbia), whereas the mountainous areas are clad in local forest types including Canary pines and laurels.

CLIMATE AND AGRICULTURE

Just as the natural vegetation is greatly influenced by the regional climates of Spain, so too is its agricultural land use. Figure 5.10 shows two climatic factors which severely limit agriculture (see also Figure 5.8, the pattern of agricultural land use in Spain).

Some of the main features to note are:
- The distinctive economy of the Atlantic zone where green pastures, dairy herds, apple orchards and high hedges are similar in appearance to South Wales or the West Country – regions with similar climates.
- The relationship between the Meseta and cereal production. Limited rainfall, high summer temperatures, but cold winters favour extensive cereal production, which has been the traditional economy of this region.

- Tree crops, especially olives and cork oaks, still predominate in the dry, inland areas of Andalusia and Extremadura, reflecting the pattern of natural vegetation.
- The irrigated areas of the Mediterranean coast and the inland river valleys are the most productive agricultural areas of Spain. Sheltered but lacking rainfall, these are highly productive for vines, fruits and vegetables, once they are irrigated. In areas such as around Almería, greenhouse production of early high-value vegetables and exotic fruits takes advantage of high insolation rates (approximately 3000 sunshine hours per annum) as well as local irrigation water.
- The Canary Islands with their unique quasi-tropical climate can produce crops such as bananas, which are not grown successfully out of doors in mainland Spain.

A CHANGING CLIMATE?

Drought and water supply have always imposed problems for Spain and its agriculture. In the mid 1990s, however, there were several winters where rainfall totals for most of Spain were less than 50 per cent of the seasonal average; Andalusia and other southern regions were the most badly affected. These same parts of Spain are undergoing rapid growth in tourism infrastructure (hotels, swimming pools, golf courses), which has produced conflicts with local farmers over water supplies.

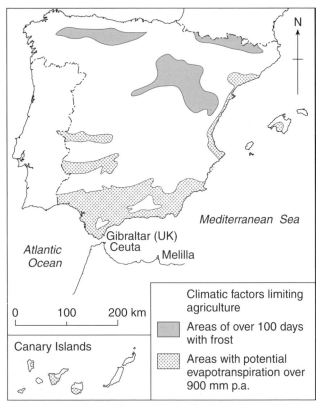

Figure 5.10 *Climatic factors limiting agriculture*

To what extent any changes in rainfall pattern are just short-term and, indeed, typical of a semi-arid climate, or more long-term and due to global climate change, it is not yet possible to say.

Figure 5.12 *Farmers demonstrating in Seville over water shortage*

Figure 5.11 *Bananas and volcano, Gran Canaria*

SUMMARY

- Great diversity of regional climates
- Second most mountainous country in Europe
- Large Iberian land mass of 596 800 km^2
- Strong relationship between east–west trending mountains and rainfall
- Influenced by the same five air masses as UK
- Atlantic region has 1000+ mm of rainfall; Meseta less than 500 mm.
- Greatest continental effect in south-east Meseta (21 °C)
- Least continental effect in Vigo (10 °C) and the Canaries (8 °C)
- Canaries have unique local climate due to latitude
- Climate classification into 11 regions
- Strong relationships between climate and natural vegetation:
  NW to SE changes from deciduous forest through Mediterranean forest to scrubland
- Agricultural pattern determined by climate: Atlantic, Meseta and Mediterranean agricultural areas; importance of irrigation.

 EXAMINATION QUESTIONS

This case study deals specifically with the distribution of climatic belts within one country, but it may have wider applications in relating climate to ecosystems and to human activities, particularly agriculture.

SPECIFIC

Examples of questions which have a direct bearing on the case study material:

1 With reference to one or more countries you have studied, explain why there may be large variations in climate within relatively short distances.
2 For any country you have studied, suggest how it may be subdivided into climatic zones. Justify the basis on which these subdivisions have been made.

GENERAL

More general questions which could use this case study, especially in combination with others could include:

3 Examine the suggestion that climate is the main factor which controls the distribution of natural vegetation, on both a large scale and a small scale.
4 'In some countries climate is a more important factor in determining agricultural land use patterns than in others.' Critically examine this statement using examples of countries you have studied.

CASE STUDY 6

THE RAINFORESTS OF WEST AFRICA

... one is forced to the conclusion that the virgin forests of the country, if unprotected, will all have been exploited and agriculture, within the forest zone, will have reached its optimum within the coming generation.

T. F. Chipps, Deputy Conservator of Forests, Gold Coast (1922)

Even though this rather pessimistic prediction about Ghana's forests did not come true, deforestation has taken place at a rapid rate, leaving the tropical rainforests of West Africa in an impoverished and degraded state. Luckily, conservation schemes in most countries along the West African coast have saved at least part of the region's biogeographical heritage.

Africa, Latin America and South East Asia contain the world's three major tropical rainforest formations, yet there are great contrasts in the extent, the structure and the diversity of these three ecosystems which are separated by thousands of kilometres in distance and by hundreds of millions of years in time since the break-up of the supercontinents; both factors have allowed them to evolve separately.

Once much more widespread than today, Africa's rainforests cover only 7 per cent of the continent (cf. 37 per cent in South America). It is mainly restricted to two areas – the lowlands along the Guinea Coast and the much more extensive but less densely populated heart of Africa drained by the River Congo and its tributaries. (Figure 6.1 shows the past and current extent of African rainforests.)

In comparison with the other two formations, African rainforest has far fewer species. So far, between 7500 and 8000 species have been identified or recorded in the forests of Africa, yet in the comparatively small area of Malaysia there are over 8500 species. Several theories have been put forward to explain these differences, although it must be understood that the African forests, especially in the Congo, have been less well-explored and documented than elsewhere.

One possible explanation is climatic change and that during the Pleistocene, long periods of cold, dry conditions could have caused the extinction of many species. Another suggestion has been the long history of human occupation in Africa together with the use of fire; this may have had a negative effect on the continent's biodiversity. A third explanation is in the fairly flat, low-lying topography of Central and Western Africa, which would allow certain species to propagate over large areas without interruption, thereby excluding less successful species. The African rainforest may be poorer in its plant diversity than the other associations, but it is much richer in its number of primate species; these two factors may, indeed, be related.

THE NATURE OF THE ECOSYSTEM

The tropical rainforest is the most productive of the world's biomes, because of the optimum climatic conditions experienced in the equatorial regions: an abundant rainfall, with almost constantly high humidity and temperatures. Within West Africa,

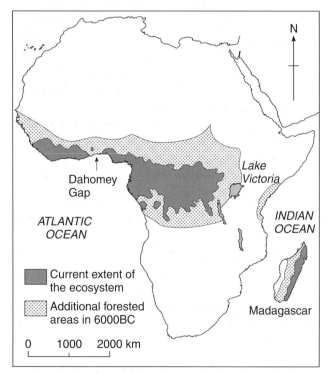

Figure 6.1 *The extent of the African rainforest today and in 6000 BC*

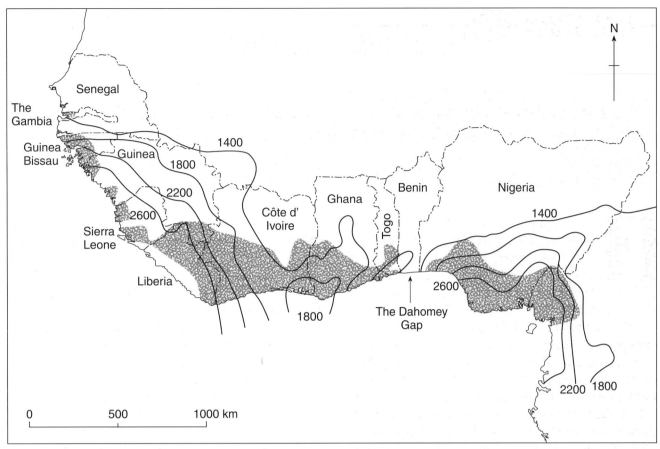

Figure 6.2 *The extent of the rainforest ecosystem within the countries of West Africa*

however, there are considerable variations in both rainfall total and rainfall distribution, which in turn lead to variations within the actual forest associations. For example, Ghana has four major distinctive types of rainforest according to local rainfall totals, which will be considered later. Studies of the West African forests have tended to be carried out on a national basis, so it is often difficult to make comparisons between English and French speaking former colonies where the terminology and the methods of forest classification are totally different. (Figure 6.2 shows the countries of West Africa, the extent of the forest biome within them and the rainfall distribution for the region.)

Despite these variations, some general points can be made which tend to be true of the West African forests as a whole.

● The underlying soils are generally thin, poor and either clayey or acidic, having developed upon the ancient crystalline bedrock of the North West African craton. The acidic acrisols and kaolinised lixisols are the two dominant soils of the region.

● Dead organic matter (DOM) accumulates in thick quantities throughout the year on the forest floor from trees which continuously shed their leaves.

● Earthworms play only a limited role in the churning over of the soil, despite their large size in this region; bacteria, beetles, termites and millipedes are more important forms of soil biota.

● Root systems tend to be shallow, rarely deeper than 10 m, as plants take their nutrients from the DOM rather than the weathered bedrock. This often necessitates buttress root systems to support the taller vascular plants.

● Some plants such as the climbing lianes and epiphytes, such as orchids, are so efficient at their absorption of minerals, including nitrogen, that they do not need to be rooted in the ground.

The so-called 'closed forests' of West Africa, which are found in the places with the highest rainfall (over 1500 mm per annum), typically have four layers of vegetation – although local variations can be found in which there may be fewer or more levels within the forest structure. The availability of light and the ability to seek it out are the key to what grows where in the rainforest. The four typical layers are:

1 At the top of the forest are the 'emergent trees', 40 to 50 m in height, which grow up beyond the

Figure 6.3 *General view in the West African rainforest*

main canopies in order to acquire the maximum amount of light.

2 The upper canopy layer is much more uniform, at around 30 m. Here there is an almost continuous cover of leaves where tree crowns of the dominant species interlock and exclude as much as 90 per cent of the sunlight from penetrating any further down.

3 The lower canopy layer is far less uniform and includes a wide variety of medium height trees, large bushes and saplings of the taller species. Ferns, palms and a huge number of fruit trees are part of this zone's exceptional biodiversity.

4 The forest floor level is often referred to as a 'land of eternal twilight' because as little as 1 per cent of the sunlight may reach it. Ferns and woody shrubs are typical species of this zone; grasses are generally absent unless there is a large break in the canopy cover.

Within this setting, various plant species have adapted to be opportunistic. Pioneer species will not germinate unless there is sufficient light. Trees are constantly dying and collapsing, and their sunlight

niches in the forest are quickly taken by new emergents, at the same time the dead trunk becomes the host of numerous saprophytes. As with the other rainforests of the world, Africa has various species of strangler fig which entangle themselves in a host tree that is eventually killed. The strangler figs then take the tree's light space within the forest.

In contrast to the closed forests, West Africa has various forms of 'open forest', in which vegetation cover is not as dense, more light penetrates the forest floor allowing dense undergrowth to develop and many of the tree species may be deciduous. Such forests are associated either with lower total annual rainfall (less than 1500 mm) or a dry season which lasts too long to support a totally evergreen ecosystem.

Much of the West African coastline experiences the 'double maximum' rainfall regime associated with the equatorial climate and, therefore, supports a closed forest system. However, in the central and northern parts of most countries, rainforest gives way to savanna and the open forest represents a transition between the two. Only Liberia falls totally within the closed forest climatic zone.

Another climatic feature of West Africa is the 'Dahomey Gap', a coastal belt which experiences an anomalously low rainfall for the area (less then 750 mm per annum). This affects the southern parts of Togo and Benin as well as south-east Ghana; all these places have open rather than closed forests.

FOREST TYPES IN GHANA

Figure 6.4 shows a theoretical cross section through Ghana and the four distinctive types of forest which characterise the country; Figure 6.5 shows the extent of these forest types, indicating that botanists have identified further subdivisions within the classification. Each forest type is related to a specific rainfall range and has its distinctive associations of plants.

1 **Wet Evergreen Forest**
   This is found along the south-west coastal zone of Ghana, where the double maximum rainfall regime brings at least 1750 mm of rain per annum, and in places over 2000 mm. This is the most closed rainforest, with the greatest diversity of species (over 200 types of vascular plant, in a 25 × 25 m plot). Canopies are found around the 40 m level. The main tree species growing here are not common in the other types of forest, and few of them are of much importance to the timber industry.

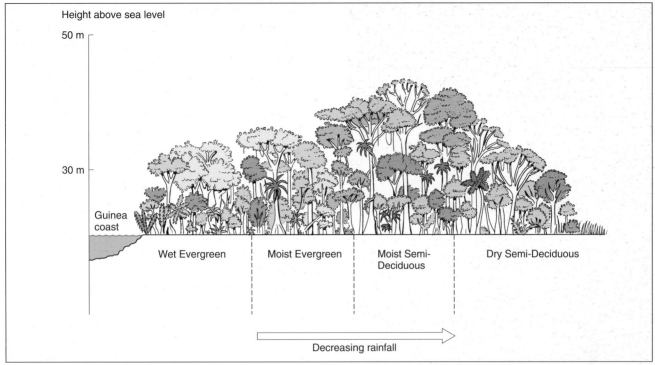

Figure 6.4 *Idealised cross section through Ghana*

2 Moist Evergreen Forest

This type of forest coincides with the 1500 to 1750 mm rainfall belt. Generally a closed type of forest, there are more gaps in the canopy layer than in the Wet Evergreen type. There is less diversity of vegetation type, with 170 species of vascular plant in a 25 × 25 m plot. Trees reach around 45 m and many of them are of great importance to the timber trade, including sapele, teak and obeche.

3 Moist Semi-Deciduous Forest

This occurs where there is a rainfall of between 1250 and 1500 mm per annum. This is the most widespread forest type not only in Ghana, but also in the whole of West Africa. The species diversity here is around 100 vascular plants per 25 × 25 m plot. Some trees grow up to 60 m in height, and this zone is not only a major one for timber production (mahogany, sapele, makore), but also the most ideal one for plantation crops and shifting cultivation.

4 Dry Semi-Deciduous Forest

Here the rainfall is generally less than 1250 mm per year and can be as low as 1000 mm, the absolute minimum to be able to support tropical forest. The trees may grow to a height of 30 to 40 m but canopies rarely interlock. Species diversity may be as low as 40 vascular plants per 25 × 25 m plot, yet there are important timberwoods such as ebony, a species associated with the savanna. Indeed, there are many species in common with the savanna which it borders and, owing to the existence of a marked dry season, fires tend to be part of the natural sequence of events in this forest type.

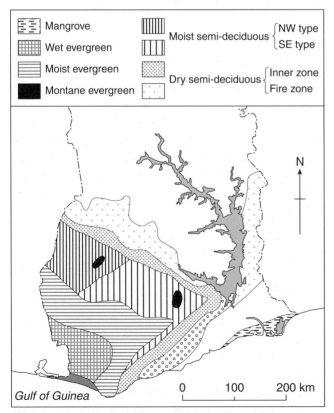

Figure 6.5 *Distribution of forest types in Ghana*

Figure 6.6 *Elmina Fort, Cape Coast, Ghana*

EUROPEAN DISCOVERY AND THE BEGINNINGS OF EXPLOITATION

The once densely forested Guinea Coast of Africa stretches for some 600 km, from Senegal in the west to Gabon in the south-east. Being closer to Europe than either South America or South East Asia, it was the first zone of tropical rainforest to be found and exploited by the great trading nations at the time of the Voyages of Discovery. Trade with the shores of the Gulf of Guinea goes back to the second half of the 15th century, when the Portuguese navigators were rounding Africa and mapping its coastline, in search of a new route to the Far East. During the 16th, 17th and 18th centuries trading posts were set up by the British, French, Dutch, Portuguese, Spanish and Danes, and their main exports were gold, ivory, slaves and timber. Along the coastline of the Gold Coast, present-day Ghana, alone there are the remains of 16 forts and castles built by the European powers to protect their trading posts and store their goods.

The abolition of the slave trade in the early 19th century indirectly led to the first comprehensive exploitation of the forests and their products, because the European powers had to find alternative sources of income to the trade in human beings. Gum from the Daniellia tree was used as a resource for making varnish and the Futumia tree yielded a type of rubber. Both of these products were greatly in demand in the late 19th century, but their exploitation was not particularly destructive to the rainforest. It was the advent of the plantation system of agriculture that spurred on deforestation from the 1880s onwards; this coincided with the 'Scramble for Africa' during which the European powers extended their colonial territories from the coasts and carved up the African interior between them.

The first major plantation product was palm oil, the growing of which led to the development of export-oriented agriculture within the countries along the West African coast. This, together with other plantation-based export crops such as bananas and cacao, has been responsible for widespread deforestation in West Africa in both the colonial and post-colonial eras.

The period of maximum exploitation was, in fact, the time which followed the independence of the West African states, when new types of machinery made timber felling in some remoter forest areas much easier. The three decades from 1950 to 1980 were the 'boom years' for the timber trade in Africa. Nowhere was more affected by this than Côte d'Ivoire, where in the period between 1972 and 1982 its annual timber exports mounted to 5 million cubic metres, or Nigeria, where all remaining virgin rainforest had been removed by the 1980s, partly to pay off huge debts incurred from the unsuccessful management of the country's oil boom. Such rates of exploitation are not compatible with sustainable development. Nigeria remains in a state of enormous environmental degradation and Côte d'Ivoire had to declassify some of its forest reserves before a dramatic slump in its timber trade reflected that supplies were becoming exhausted. (Figure 6.7 shows timber production for certain West African countries during the period of peak exploitation.)

THE ORIGINS OF FOREST CONSERVATION

Conservation of both the flora and fauna in the tropical rainforests has been part of a long tradition in West Africa and can be found within the 'indigenous laws' of the local peoples. Animist cultures believe that humans have a mystical relationship with plants, animals and natural objects such as rocks and, therefore, tribal customs, practices and taboos have tended to be protective of the natural forest environment. In some parts of the region, the forests have within them 'sacred groves' attached to villages where rituals connected to respecting of the ancestors take place; carved wooden stools represent the resting places of the forefathers. From an early time the European colonialists respected the importance of the groves and they were not exploited for timber.

In the early 20th century, the colonial governments took an active interest in the forests for both economic and scientific reasons. Various forestry departments set up by the Europeans would survey, manage, exploit and conserve the rich resources of the rainforests, with various degrees of consultation with local tribal chiefs and

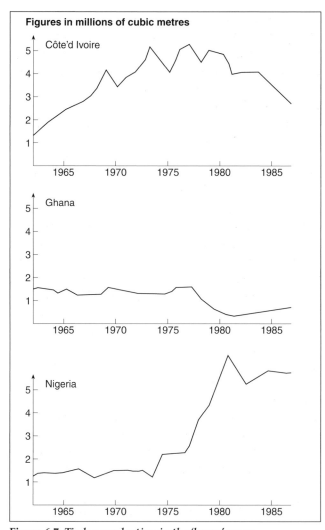

Figures in millions of cubic metres

Côte'd Ivoire

Ghana

Nigeria

Figure 6.7 *Timber production in the 'boom' years*

Four years later the Tāi National Park was set up in the same country and, with 3300 km² of protected land, remains the largest and most important protected rainforest location in West Africa.

THE EXPLOITATION AND CONSERVATION OF GHANA'S FORESTS

Ghana occupies a central position along the Gulf of Guinea, where it has 565 km of coastline. A country of 238 537 km², it has considerable variations in climate and vegetation (as already mentioned above and shown in Figure 6.5). The northern part of the country falls within the savanna belt, the south-western coastlands were originally covered in closed rainforest, whereas the south-west with its much lower rainfall comes within the 'Dahomey Gap', where natural vegetation is semi-deciduous forest.

Ghana, like all other countries in West Africa, has an active conservation policy, yet there are many land use conflicts involving the rainforest areas. Ghana has had a long history of human habitation; its first settlers, thousands of years ago, were forest dwellers who were predominantly hunters with agriculture as a dietary supplement. As the population increased over the centuries, there was greater demand on the forest produce and, therefore, agriculture increased in importance. As agriculture became more widespread, more of the forest had to be cleared, although ecologically sound forms of shifting cultivation were generally practised.

Hunting today continues to provide an important protein supplement to what is often the rather starchy Ghanaian diet for villagers; 75 per cent of the country's population still regard 'bushmeat' as a great delicacy. Monkeys, mongoose, porcupines, anteaters and cane rats are not only widely hunted in rural areas, but also fetch high prices in the urban markets. Bushmeat, along with wild vegetables and

villagers. Policies differed between administrations; for example, the British in Nigeria adopted a reafforestation strategy in 1910, only to replace it with a more realistic conservation of existing forest resources a few decades later. Generally speaking, the British (and the Germans in Togo) were from the start more conservation-minded than the French.

Conservation in Ghana (then the Gold Coast), started in 1911 with a Forestry Ordinance, which put all uninhabited forest into reserve status. This led to a lot of conflict between the colonial authorities and tribal chiefs, yet by 1939, 19 per cent of Ghana's area was protected forest reserve. France followed suit in Côte d'Ivoire and its other colonies, but all along the Guinea coast it was difficult to prevent illegal farming and other infringements into the forest reserves.

Despite the long history of conservation, it was not until 1968 that the first strictly rainforest national park was set up in West Africa; this was the small Mont Peko National Park in Côte d'Ivoire.

Figure 6.8 *Cacao trees in fruit, one of Ghana's main export crops*

fruits, nuts, oils, spices, resins and traditional medicines are all categorised as 'secondary products' of the forest, as opposed to timber, the main 'primary product'.

The continued exploitation of secondary products by villagers has had very little detrimental effect upon the forests, as levels of extraction have thus far been well within the limits of sustainability. It has been the large-scale European-instituted projects exploiting timber and setting up plantations which have caused the widespread damage to the rainforests, and have made intervention necessary.

The British colonial administration set up a Forestry Department in 1901, and since then it has changed its name and powers on numerous occasions. Since 1985 as well as a Forestry Commission, forestry has also come under two other government bodies: the Forest Products Inspection Bureau, which deals more with conservation, and the Timber Export Development Board, which is more concerned with exploitation. Ghana, like most other LEDCs, has economic problems and has to use its natural resources to the full in order to prosper. The country has had a turbulent history since its independence in 1956, with military governments, coups and counter coups, together with periods of great corruption. The country's present stability, appears to be changing its economic fortunes, through a number of Economic Recovery Programmes (ERPs).

Cocoa is still Ghana's main crop, covering 50 per cent of cultivated land and accounting for 65 per cent of the country's export earnings; no other crop has been as responsible for deforestation. Since the 1970s, all has not been well in the cocoa industry. There were serious droughts in 1976, 1977 and 1982, which led to a drop in production; at the same time the various chocolate-making multinationals managed to engineer a long-term decline in the cost of their raw materials (the cacao bean), although this now seems to be reversing.

With the decline of cocoa exports, more pressure is now back upon timber production. In 1989 timber accounted for $US 88 million of export earnings, but this grew to $US 230 million by 1994, making it Ghana's third most important commodity after cocoa and bauxite. Alongside this increase in timber output, there has been a decline in replanting in the forests; in the 1970s, this was being done at a rate of 11 000 ha per year, whereas by the early 1990s it had declined to just 4 000 ha per year. A country which was one of the first in West Africa to take

conservation seriously now seems to be backtracking, out of economic necessity. The other threat that is presented to Ghana's forests, in common with those in so many other LEDCs, is population growth and the demand for new farmland for cultivation. With a natural increase of 2.9 per cent per annum, Ghana has to feed over half a million additional people each year.

Estimates suggest that, projecting current rates of exploitation, forest reserves in Ghana will last until 2030. Concern about the rates of deforestation has recently led the World Bank to grant Ghana $US 39 million towards the conservation of its rainforests. (Figure 6.9 shows the way in which the total forest area in Ghana has declined.)

Year	Km²
1900	87 000
1950	42 000
1995	13 000

Figure 6.9 *Decline in rainforest cover in Ghana*

Ghana's long history of conservation has made considerable impact on the environment. Protected areas now account for 16 per cent of the country's total area; these fall into four main categories:

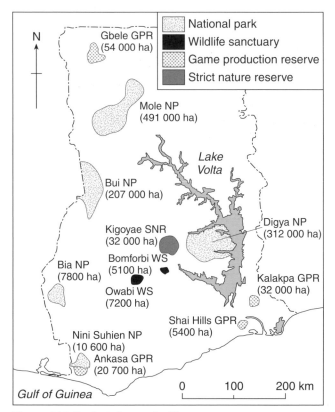

Figure 6.10 *Protected areas in Ghana*

National Parks, Strict Nature Reserves, Wildlife Sanctuaries and Game Protection Reserves (see Figure 6.10). Some of these parks may be small, but they are preserving many disappearing plant and animal species. The Forestry Commission is the main government body responsible for conservation, together with Ghana Association for Conservation of Nature (GACON), a voluntary organisation.

The main constraints placed upon the work of these and other conservation bodies, are those commonly experienced in LEDCs. There are problems in recruitment, staffing shortages, lack of funds, poor salaries and living conditions, lack of proper management skills, shortage of scientific data and ill-defined boundaries between protected and non-protected areas. Above all, there are conflicts of interest in Ghana, as in the other countries of West Africa, between large organisations and local people, between traditional practices and modern forms of land use, between conservationists and exploiters, and between the need to develop and the need to preserve.

SUMMARY

- Rainforest covers only 7 per cent of Africa
- The African forests are less biodiverse than those in Asia and South America
- They also have a very long period of human use
- In a cross section through Ghana there are four distinctive forest types
- The Dahomey Gap is an unforested area of lower rainfall
- The African rainforest was the first to be exploited by Europeans
- Logging, plantations and shifting cultivation are the main threats
- Nigeria's logging policy was much less conservative than Ghana's
- Ghana has a wide variety of protected areas
- The decline of cocoa has become a new threat in Ghana
- Ghana's forests have declined from 88 000 to 14 000 km^2 since 1900

 EXAMINATION QUESTIONS

This case study lends itself both to the specifically physical environment type question as well as to the destruction of the ecosystem.

SPECIFIC

Specific questions may include:
1 Choosing any one of the world's major biomes, examine how its vegetation is adapted to the local environmental conditions.
2 Examine the nature of the tropical rainforest as an example of a high-productivity ecosystem.

GENERAL

More general questions could include:
3 With reference to a region which you have studied, examine the changes which are taking place today within the tropical rainforest.
4 What are the main pressures imposed upon the world's major ecosystems? Illustrate your answer with specific examples from countries which you have studied.

— CASE STUDY — ⑦ SOIL EROSION AND LAND DEGRADATION IN BASILICATA

Some regions are more erodable than others... So far as Mediterranean Europe is concerned, each year 60 to 600 tonnes of material per km² might be in the process of removal from the land, to find its way to the coast and out into the sea basins.

Catherine Delano-Smith

Most of Southern Italy falls into Delano-Smith's 'more erodable' category, but no region bears such extreme scars of soil erosion as Basilicata. This region, which occupies the 'instep' of peninsular Italy's 'boot' is in many respects the nation's poorest region. Large parts of Basilicata have an almost 'lunar' landscape made up of heavily gullied hillsides, badlands and hummocky relic hills – the products of soil erosion and land degradation which have been allowed to take place, largely unchecked, for over 2000 years. During that time, the physical factors of geology, relief and climate together with population pressure, deforestation and poor land management, have held back Basilicata's economic development. It is a region which still relies heavily upon agriculture, where people live in large, overpopulated hilltop villages, where unemployment is well above the national average and where emigration is the easiest solution to economic problems.

RELIEF, GEOLOGY AND SOILS

A region of 9992 km², Basilicata has a 20 km coastline along the Tyrrehenian Sea and a 40 km coastline along the Gulf of Taranto, part of the Ionian Sea. The region is mountainous in the north and west, dropping down to undulating hill-country towards the Ionian Sea. The only extensive area of flat land is along the Gulf of Taranto. Italian geographers classify Basilicata as 47 per cent mountains, 45 per cent hills and 8 per cent plain. (See Figure 7.1.)

Most of peninsular Italy, including Basilicata, is geologically young. Its rocks are mainly sedimentary strata laid down as marine deposits during the Tertiary and Quaternary eras (between 25 million years ago and the present). In the west are the higher mountains, such as Monte Pollino, made of more resistant limestones, whereas in the south

and east the hill-country is composed of softer sediments such as sands, clays and marls. There is often complex interbedding of permeable and impermeable strata within these deposits which is one of the main reasons for their instability. In the north of Basilicata is the volcanic Monte Vulture, from which igneous rocks are spread over a 20 km radius of its caldera.

The soils of Basilicata reflect the parent material from which they have developed. On the highest

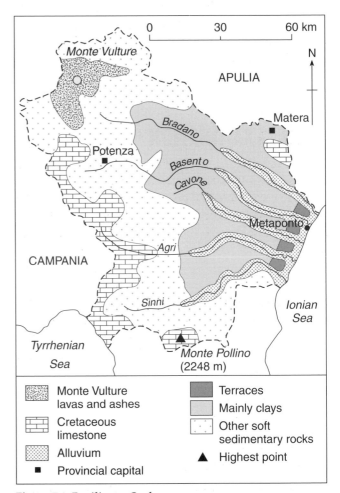

Figure 7.1 *Basilicata: Geology*

exposed limestone peaks there are lithosols. Elsewhere on the limestone, rendzinas have developed. Richer brown earths have formed on the Monte Vulture tuffs and lavas and on parts of the Apennine foothills. The problem soils of the region, however, are those of the southern and eastern hill-country. Where clay deposits are dominant and the natural vegetation cover has been removed, the top soil is exposed to the extremes of the local climate. In the summer heat it is baked hard and huge surface cracks appear; in the winter rains it becomes waterlogged and mobile.

CLIMATE AND HYDROLOGY

Basilicata has a wide temperature range; its summers are often dominated by three months of temperatures well over 25 °C, with dry winds blowing straight from the Sahara. By contrast, the winter brings frosts and snow; it is not unusual for temperatures to fall to –15 °C.

Most of the rainfall of the region falls during autumn and winter with depressions moving eastwards over the Mediterranean. Thus, the areas with the highest rainfall are the more elevated parts of the west. The eastern parts of the region lie in the rain shadow and the hill-country therefore has a rainfall of less than 800 mm. This rainfall is uneven; although there is a winter maximum, there is great variability from year to year and month to month. In the Basento Valley, the recorded annual total has varied from 1002 mm down to as little as 540 mm. Its number of rainfall days in the year has varied from 98 maximum to 39 minimum. Such statistics as these are bad news for soil conservationists!

Five main rivers drain 80 per cent of Basilicata: the Bradano, Basento, Cavone, Agri and Sinni, which flow out into the Ionian Sea. The River Agri was navigable in Roman times and the Sinni was navigable as late as the 13th century. This would be impossible today as centuries of erosion and deposition have left the rivers braided and clogged with sediments. Like the rainfall, the rivers' flow patterns are irregular, the summer discharge in their lower courses being negligible. The average flow into the sea during the summer drought period is as follows:

Sinni	21 cumecs
Agri	11 cumecs
Basento	10 cumecs
Bradano	8 cumecs
Cavone	ceases to flow.

In winter spate the rivers may discharge well over

Figure 7.2 *The River Sinni near Aliano*

1000 cumecs. (The highest flow recorded is that of the Basento at 2250 cumecs.) The sediment load carried by these rivers can be as great as 1000 tonnes/km in the Basento and 2500 tonnes/km in the Sinni. These huge variations in both the flow and the amount of sediment in the river channels reflect the causes and effects of erosion in the hill-country.

SETTLEMENT AND POPULATION

With a total of 623 000 people, Basilicata has the third smallest population of Italy's 20 regions. It also has one of the lowest densities (62 people per km²). Traditionally, most people lived in the large nucleated hilltop villages, which continue as the main form of settlement today. These villages may have as many as 20 000 inhabitants and are best described as *città contadine* (peasant cities). They were sited on hilltops for a combination of defence from invaders and to be away from the malaria-ridden swamps of the river valleys and coastal plains below. Of the 131 *comuni* (parishes), 75 per cent are at elevations over 400 m. These same hills are generally geologically unstable and subject to erosion and landslides. Poor road networks have left many of the villages isolated until recent decades.

Population growth in Basilicata has not been even. Natural disasters and emigration have both provided checks on a burgeoning population growth. From 1881 to 1911, the region lost 25 per cent of its population through emigration. By contrast, during the Fascist era (1922–43), when emigration was restricted by law, there was a 13 per cent population increase. Poor land quality and the tiny size of the average peasant smallholding led to poor nutrition and health which held back some of the population growth – mortality rates remained high until the 1950s.

soil erosion and land degradation in Basilicata

DEFORESTATION AND LAND USE

Basilicata once had extensive forests. The cold winters meant that much of the vegetation cover was deciduous oak forest rather than of Mediterranean evergreen oaks. The wood from the forests was prized by Greek and Roman colonists in the south, and it can be assumed that deforestation and consequent soil erosion took place from early times. Normally, short-term changes affect farmers most, but in the case of Southern Italy, long-term degradation has caused the biggest problems.

The 19th century was the greatest period of deforestation. Population growth and the demands for more cereal land were the main motives for deforestation. By 1870 the amount of woodland had been reduced to just 202 527 hectares, and by 1929 the forests had been further reduced to 125 985 hectares. In the Fascist era, Mussolini's 'Battle for Grain' planned to make Italy self-sufficient in wheat; this led to further deforestation in Basilicata and took marginal land away from rough grazing, putting it down to wheat.

Cereals do not hold the topsoil together as well as the roots of trees. Sowing of cereals on fairly steep slopes and ploughing downslope rather than around the contours were common forms of agricultural mismanagement, which merely encouraged soil erosion. Worryingly, these practices can still be seen in Basilicata today!

THE PROCESSES AND FEATURES OF EROSION

The processes of soil erosion in Basilicata are complex. The variety of erosional landscape features can be best appreciated by looking at the land around the group of villages most badly affected – Pisticci, Montalbano, Aliano and Craco (see Figure 7.3). Gully erosion will start on slopes as gentle as 15°, if the conditions are right (e.g. downslope ploughing, lack of vegetation cover). When the clayey soils are baked dry in the summer drought and their surfaces become cracked, the first heavy rains of the autumn can infiltrate through the cracks and reduce the topsoil to a slurry, creating mudflows and *calanchi* (large gullies). Seismic instability in the region also helps to trigger mudflows and landslides. The four villages named above have all lost rows of houses over their hillsides during periods of heavy rain, and Craco was actually abandoned in 1975 following severe landslides. The overgrown village of Pisticci is

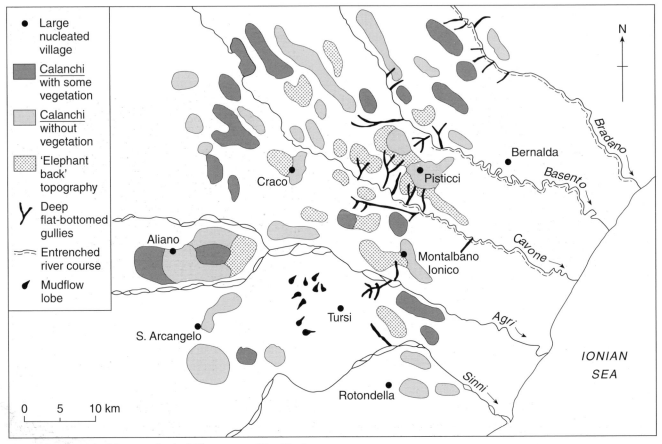

Figure 7.3 *Erosional features in the hill-country of Basilicata*

under constant threat of further subsidence; Figure 7.5 indicates the geological background to these problems. A retaining wall has been built to prevent further subsidence in Pisticci.

Figure 7.4 *Deep erosion gullies or* **calanchi** *at the foot of the clay hills on which Montalbano is located. This area is now almost completely devoid of vegetation*

Traditionally, the lands of these villages were farmed right up the hillsides to the edges of the settlements themselves. The steepness of the slopes and the heavy gullying have meant that most farmland close to the villages has been abandoned;

Figure 7.6 shows how this has affected the land-use pattern in the Agri valley around Montalbano.

At the bottoms of the slopes, closer to the river valleys, gully erosion has been so severe that whole hillsides have been reduced to hummocky topography made up of relict hills, known in Italian as *dorsi di elefanti* (elephants' backs). Overall, the landscapes of the hill-country of Basilicata may appear to outsiders as having a wild, arid beauty – but to the local population they are a reminder of a constant battle against the forces of nature.

REMEDIAL ACTION

Following centuries of exploitation, bad management and neglect, the problems of Basilicata and its cycle of soil erosion and poverty have been dealt with only since the 1950s. The setting up of the *Cassa per il Mezzogiorno* in 1950, gave Europe its first integrated regional development plan. Basilicata has benefited greatly from the Italian government investment in South Italy and the schemes which have resulted from it.

Efforts have been made to remedy the soil erosion and land degradation problems – as well as to provide a wider framework for the development of

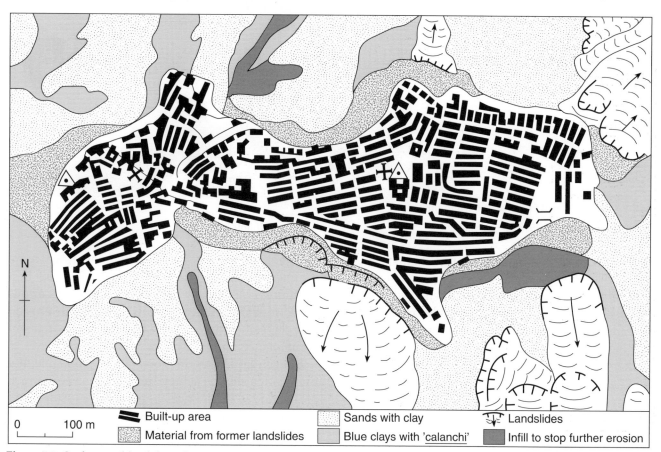

0 100 m	Built-up area	Sands with clay	Landslides
	Material from former landslides	Blue clays with 'calanchi'	Infill to stop further erosion

Figure 7.5 *Geology and land degradation around Pisticci*

soil erosion and land degradation in Basilicata

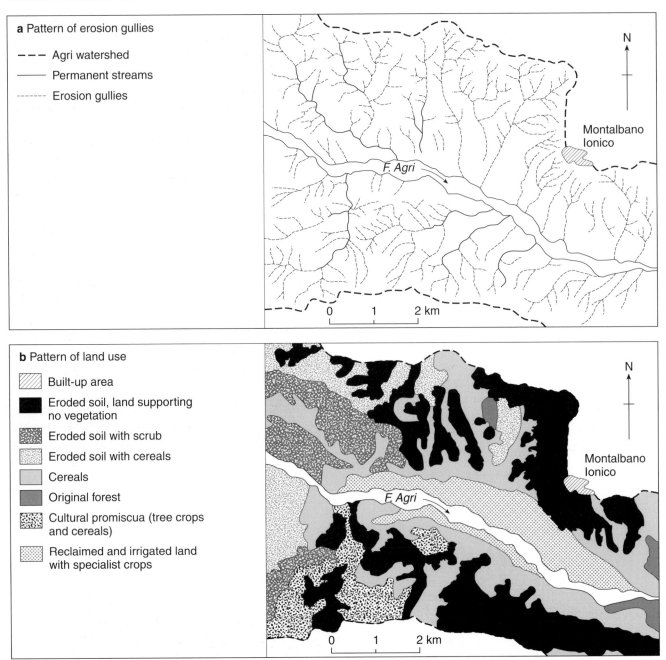

a Pattern of erosion gullies

- – – – Agri watershed
- —— Permanent streams
- - - - - Erosion gullies

Montalbano
Ionico

F. Agri

0   1   2 km

b Pattern of land use

- Built-up area
- Eroded soil, land supporting no vegetation
- Eroded soil with scrub
- Eroded soil with cereals
- Cereals
- Original forest
- Cultural promiscua (tree crops and cereals)
- Reclaimed and irrigated land with specialist crops

Montalbano
Ionico

F. Agri

0   1   2 km

Figure 7.6 *Erosion and land use near Montalbano*

a *Pattern of erosion gullies*

b *Pattern of land use*

Basilicata out of its former economic stagnation. At the local level, around the villages, a whole series of measures are being used to slow down erosion rates and to stabilise and, where possible, reclaim the degraded 'lunar' landscapes for agricultural use. (see Figure 7.7) Steep slopes which are in danger of further subsidence – as well as having retaining walls as at Pisticci, are terraced and planted with fast-growing trees and bushes such as pines and broom. (It is unlikely that these steeper slopes will ever become farmland again.)

The main problem posed by erosion gullies is that they get larger and help to channel down more sediment after each rainstorm. One of the best solutions is to create concrete silt-traps at various levels in these gullies to slow down both erosion and deposition rates. Such barriers need frequent maintenance.

On gentler slopes, reafforestation is possible, but this is often slow to achieve and expensive. So much of the eroded land, once abandoned, is just left and the processes of erosion are allowed to continue; efforts to develop the land are, therefore, concentrated elsewhere.

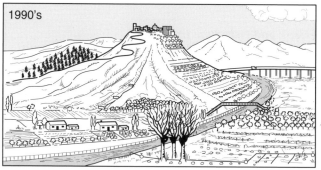

Figure 7.7 *Changes in the Basilicata landscape*

farming settlements established. A population shift from the old hilltop villages to the new farms and hamlets is being encouraged, although the older generations are reluctant to move.

In addition, there is new infrastructure – fast, new highways along the main river valleys replace the old 'spinal' roads which link the hilltop villages. In places, the rivers have been dammed to collect irrigation water, generate electricity and to control flooding. New industries and coastal resorts are being set up in new towns such as Scanzano and Metaponto, the aim of the government being to stimulate the trend away from employment in agriculture and to encourage the flow of people from hilltowns to lowlands.

The *Cassa* was wound up in 1985, but regional aid continues to come from Rome and Brussels. The lives of the people of Basilicata are changing rapidly; between 1980 and 1996, the percentage of people working on the land in Basilicata declined from 30 per cent to 21 per cent; (the Italian national average is just 9 per cent). There is still much argument in Italy as to whether the poor South will ever catch up with the rich North. However, the heavily eroded landscapes of Basilicata remain as a reminder of a much greater poverty in the past.

Thus, to compensate, large-scale development schemes and changes have been made in the river valleys and along the coastal plains of Basilicata. Marshes have been reclaimed, the land irrigated, new high-yielding crops introduced and new

Figure 7.8 *Pisticci – a typical "città contadina"*

SUMMARY

Basilicata: one of Italy's poorest regions

- 60–6000 tonnes of material lost per km
- 623 000 population
- *Temperature range* 25°C summer; –15°C winter
- *Rainfall* very variable (e.g. 540–1002 mm.)
- *River sediment loads* 1000–2500 tonnes per km
- *Erosion evidence* gullies (CALANCHI)
  elephants' backs (DORSI DI ELEFANTI)
  1950–1985 CASSA PER IL MEZZOGIORNO

- 9992 km² in area
- five main rivers into Ionian Sea: Agri, Basento, Bradano, Cavone, Sinni
- 47 per cent mountain; 45 per cent hills; 8 per cent plain.
- CITTA CONTADINE: Pisticci, Aliano, Montalbano

- *Remedies* terracing, reafforestation, silt traps; and elsewhere irrigation, new farms, new crops, new roads

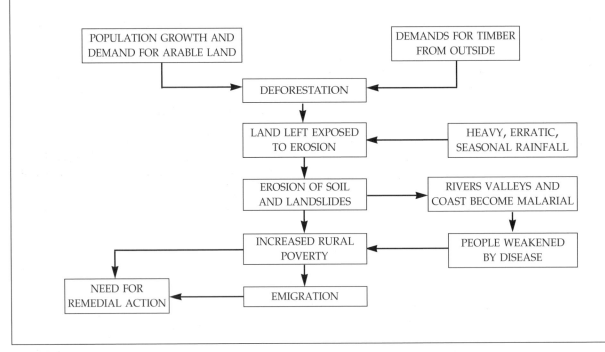

POPULATION GROWTH AND DEMAND FOR ARABLE LAND → DEFORESTATION ← DEMANDS FOR TIMBER FROM OUTSIDE

DEFORESTATION → LAND LEFT EXPOSED TO EROSION ← HEAVY, ERRATIC, SEASONAL RAINFALL

LAND LEFT EXPOSED TO EROSION → EROSION OF SOIL AND LANDSLIDES → RIVERS VALLEYS AND COAST BECOME MALARIAL

RIVERS VALLEYS AND COAST BECOME MALARIAL → PEOPLE WEAKENED BY DISEASE

EROSION OF SOIL AND LANDSLIDES → INCREASED RURAL POVERTY ← PEOPLE WEAKENED BY DISEASE

INCREASED RURAL POVERTY → NEED FOR REMEDIAL ACTION

INCREASED RURAL POVERTY → EMIGRATION → NEED FOR REMEDIAL ACTION

EXAMINATION QUESTIONS

This case study has its most direct application in answering questions on, what most Boards now call simply, 'Ecosystems'. These questions may deal with the cause and effects of soil erosion, involve the analysis of spatial patterns within an area affected by it, or a more historical/sequential approach of the reasons for and processes resulting from erosion and land degradation. The topic also has a bearing on Regional Development issues and could be used as a detailed 'cast study within a case study' if the candidate is dealing with the Italian *Mezzogiorno*. In all cases, the summary flow chart, sketch maps derived from the maps in the text, key statistics and place names need to be revised/memorised to back up the basic arguments.

SPECIFIC

Examples of specific questions connected with the 'Ecosystems' topic:

1 With reference to an area or areas you have studied, outline the ways in which both physical and human geography may contribute to the causes of soil erosion.
2 Discuss the assertion that our failure to understand the working of ecosystems has restricted success in the prevention of environmental damage.

GENERAL

More general use of this case study, in combination with others, could help to answer such questions as:

3 Why, within almost all countries, are some areas more prosperous than others?
4 With reference to specific examples you have studied, assess the importance of careful land management in areas with hazardous environments.

— CASE STUDY — **8** THE COASTLINE OF KENT

> Listen! You hear the grating roar
> Of pebbles which the waves suck back, and fling,
> At their return up the high strand,
> Begin and cease, and then again begin ...
>
> *Matthew Arnold, Dover Beach*

Kent's coastline, although it generally lacks dramatic scenery, is one of the most varied in Britain. Stretching from the Thames Estuary in the north, round to the Isle of Thanet in the east and to Dungeness in the south-west, it is one of the most densely populated sections of British coastline. This poses many environmental questions connected with the human use of the coastline, the degree to which defences from erosion are perceived as being necessary, the extent to which wildlife habitats require special protection and what the long-term consequences of sea-level change are likely to be. (Figure 8.1 shows the location of the main centres of population along the Kent coast.)

GEOLOGICAL BACKGROUND

The Kent coastline's varied scenery is the result of a combination of factors including geology, winds, tides, geomorphological processes, sea-level change

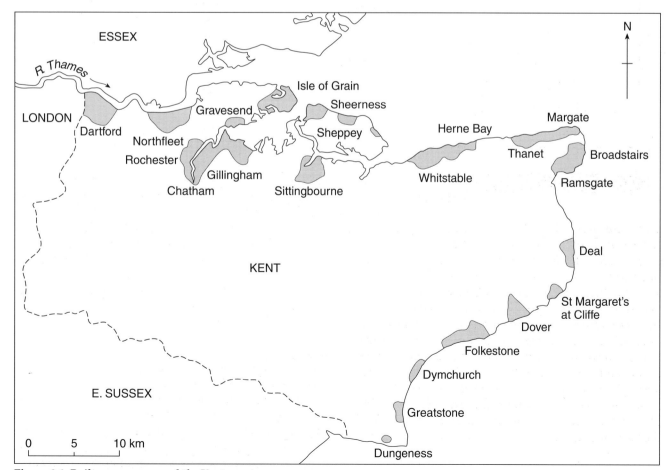

Figure 8.1 *Built-up areas around the Kent coast*

the coastline of Kent

and human interference. Geologically, the whole area is quite young for the British Isles, having been formed in the last 144 million years and, therefore, in general is built up from non-resistant materials which are readily eroded by the sea. The most striking exception to this rule is, however, the white chalk cliffs for which the county is famous. (Figure 8.2 shows the main geological foundations of the county.)

Around the Isle of Thanet and between Kingsdown and Folkestone, vertical cliffs up to 130 m in height dominate the shoreline. Where local variations in geology determine, all the classic landforms associated with the erosion of cliffs and headlands are present: caves, geos, sea-arches, stacks, stumps and wave-cut platforms.

Elsewhere in the county, where cliffs occur, they are made of softer, less resistant materials and, therefore, lack the vertical profiles of the chalk formations. Three types of more erodable cliffs can be identified.

● Folkestone Warren is a 5-km stretch of coastline where the Cretaceous chalk cliffs overlie Gault Clay. Where and when the clay becomes saturated, slumping occurs in the cliffs which gives them a stepped profile. In places these cliffs are 140 m high.

● Around Whitstable, on the Isle of Sheppey and on the Isle of Grain, there are much lower cliffs (up to 60 m high) in the London Clay deposits. The incoherence of this material leads to the saturation of certain layers and consequent slumping. Such cliffs are extremely unstable.

● Around Reculver, the London Clay is capped with glacial drift deposits. Once again, slumping is widespread in the 30 m cliffs and is merely accelerated by the local variations in geology.

All of these cliff-lined areas are subject to marine erosion, the effectiveness of which depends greatly upon the orientation of the coastline (north-facing coasts being the most vulnerable), and to the frequency of storm surges, during which most damage is done.

Away from the cliff-lined coasts, the land is low lying, corresponding to areas of deposition where the shoreline has been advancing in historical times, for which there is plenty of archaeological and cartographic evidence.

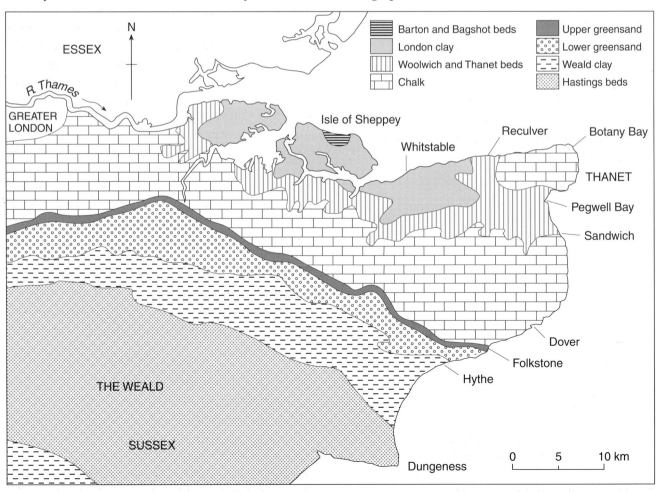

Figure 8.2 *Geological structure of Kent*

Dungeness is the most important of the depositional features, being the largest cuspate foreland in Europe. Formed by a complex pattern of sediment movement, its shingle ridges extended far enough to cut what is now Romney Marsh off from the English Channel, of which it was once an inlet.

Unlike other parts of the British coastline, there are few areas of sand dunes in Kent, the two main locations where sea and wind conditions are right for their development are to be found on the north side of Dungeness and along what is now the golf courses between Richborough and Deal.

Elsewhere there are extensive areas of saltmarsh, where lower lying shorelines protected from the excesses of storm surges have built up into intertidal mud flats which have been colonised by marine halophytes such as common saltmarsh-grass and sea lavender. Some of the most significant marshes are found on the south side of the Isle of Sheppey, the north side of the Isle of Grain within the Thames estuary and within the estuary of the River Medway. (Figure 8.3 on page 64 plots the main geomorphological features of the Kent coast.)

WIND, WAVES AND WATER

The coastline of Kent is comparatively sheltered for British shores. Winds exceed a speed of 15 m per second for only 0.1 per cent of the time. Localised variations in topography and the trend of the coast influence wind direction, the degree of exposure to storms and strength of their impact. The wind rose for Margate (Figure 8.4) shows that the north-easterly is the dominant wind. All parts of the Kent coast are sheltered from the prevailing south-westerlies which create the rapid coastal erosion rates in such places as the West Country, Wales and Western Scotland. Even the easterly and north-easterly winds are slow to influence the coastline because the fetch across the Straits of Dover is a mere 50 km and the fetch across to the northern coast of Kent from the Low Countries is some 200 km. East Anglia protects the north Kent coast from northerly winds.

In all cases, whatever the wind direction, the maximum impact of winds and waves upon the coast is achieved under storm conditions. Storm surges of different heights occur at different intervals; for example, the typical 50-year surge leads to seas which are 2.5 m above normal levels in the Thames estuary, but only 2.25 m higher in Ramsgate and 2.0 m at Dungeness. Under such conditions, several years or even decades worth of erosion and deposition may occur in a few days.

The movement of marine sediments is determined by the exposure of coasts to the various winds. Figure 8.3 shows how this happens around the Kent coastline. Along the northern coast which has maximum exposure to the north-easterlies there is a general movement to the west, similar to parallel coastlines elsewhere in Britain. The impact of the north-easterly winds also causes longshore drift southwards down the east coast of Thanet. However, most of the south coast has an eastward movement due to the mild but significant influence of the south-westerlies. The situation is most complex on the east side of Dungeness, where the longshore drift may be in either direction.

THE ISLE OF THANET AND RECULVER

An indication of the changes which have taken place along the coast of Kent in historic times can be seen from the map of the Roman shoreline (Figure 8.5.). The Isle of Thanet was at that time a real island, a chalk outlier of the North Downs. The River Stour was a coastal creek which enabled Roman Canterbury to be a seaport. The coastal fort at Richborough now lies 4 km from the old shoreline, showing how fast the rates of sedimentation have been. By contrast, the Roman fort on the North Kent coast at Reculver has been partly destroyed by erosive wave action. Figure 8.6 shows how rapidly the cliffs are receding (up to

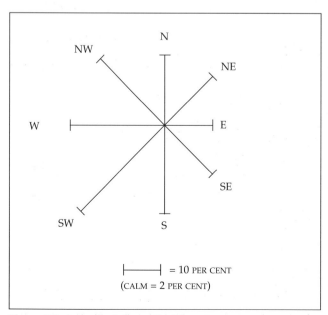

Figure 8.4 Annual wind rose for Margate

the coastline of Kent

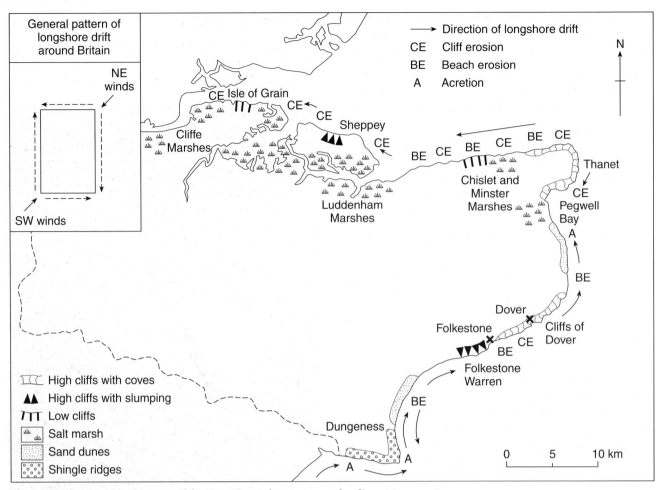

Figure 8.3 *Geomorphical areas and features; Coastal processes and sediment transport*

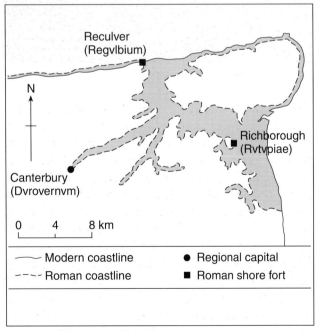

Figure 8.5 *The Roman shoreline*

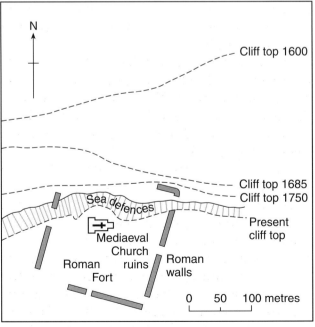

Figure 8.6 *Cliff recession at Reculver*

250 m in 400 years) and is based on evidence from historic maps. The historic complex of Roman walls and the ruins of the mediaeval church are now protected from further erosion by massive concrete containing sea-walls and huge boulders which dissipate some of the power of the pounding storm waves.

Around the chalk cliff coast of Thanet, there is an intricate pattern of coves, bays and headlands. The rocks are mostly horizontal bedded and well jointed, which has influenced both the cliff profiles (they are mainly near-vertical) and the way in which the rocks are eroded. Along the north Thanet coast where erosion would be most rapid because of the north-easterly winds, the highly urbanised shoreline of Margate is made up almost entirely from concrete sea-walls. The cliffs here are low (up to around 25 m), but the wave-cut platforms are very wide, indicating how much cliff recession has taken place in the past.

The least artificially controlled stretch of the Thanet coast is where it is less urbanised around North Foreland and Botany Bay. The cliff base is pitted with rectangular and trapezoidal caves, their shapes determined by the blocky structure of the chalk, and they are up to 3 m high and 5 m deep. Most of the erosion is carried out at high tide during storm surges. The combination of cave formation and the creation of dry valleys in areas of structural weakness had led to the development of deep, gorge-like incisions or 'geos' which appear as gaps in the cliff-line.

Where the orientation of the coastline has led to the creation of headlands, sea-arches and stacks have formed; at White Ness to the north of North Foreland there is a sea-arch and in Botany Bay is a stack which resulted from the recent collapse of a well-developed arch.

Wave-cut platforms average 200 to 300 m in width at normal low tide. The cliff recession which creates them varies considerably from one part of Thanet to another, and can be as much as 5 m per annum on exposed headlands, to much less than 1 m in the more protected bays and coves. As wave-cut platforms get wider, they help to protect the shoreline from further erosion, except during the heaviest storms. Research on these platforms has shown that they have concave upper slopes and convex lower slopes, which is likely to be due to the fact that most erosion takes place during storm surges.

THE ISLE OF SHEPPEY

The Isle of Sheppey provides a sharp contrast with the Thanet area. Separated from the North Kent mainland by a narrow, muddy channel known as

Figure 8.7 *Sea-arch at Botany Bay*

The Swale, the island is some 15 km long by 7 km wide the southern half of Sheppey is flat, low lying, mainly uninhabited and most of it is either marshland or pasture reclaimed from the marshland. The north side of the island is made from deposits of London Clay which have been moulded into a gently undulating landscape, reaching 73 m at its highest point. Along this north coast the clay forms unstable cliffs of varying heights, close to which are located a large number of permanent and holiday homes. Sheerness, Minster and Leysdown-on-Sea are the main resort towns, but in between them there are large areas taken up by holiday camps and caravan sites, often precariously near to the cliff edges.

Soft cliffs such as these are prone to weather back as a result of rain action, experience surface

the coastline of Kent

Figure 8.8 *Groynes near Herne Bay*

cracking, undergo mass movement by rotational slumping as rainwater infiltrates the clay, as well as being attacked by 'toe erosion' from the sea. The rates of cliff recession are greatest during wet, stormy winter months, during which marine action and rotational slumping are both potentially high. Mudflows and, where wave action has created overhangs, cliff falls, are also common along the north Sheppey coast. Although some areas have been provided with groynes to slow down the rates of longshore sediment movement, they have had little impact upon impeding cliff recession. The actual rates of erosion depend on cliff height,

weather conditions and human activity (e.g. wastewater disposal which may add to the amount of groundwater in the clay).

In 1979, a number of caravans were lost over the edge of the 50 m high stepped cliffs at Boarers Run, near Minster. This led to a study and report from the Borough Engineer on the stability of Sheppey's northern coastline. The report identified six problem areas, which are shown in Figure 8.9. Some of these places already had groynes or other types of sea defences, although these structures were proving to be of limited value. The engineer had to weigh up the cost benefits of any new sea defences, which would be funded by local taxpayers, against the number of permanent home properties which were in danger by being too close to the receding shoreline.

At only two of the six locations was expenditure on new sea defences recommended; in both of these places there are more permanent homes than caravans. At The Leas, Minster, where the beach was already well groyned there were found to be severe cracks in the clay cliffs, which were also being undermined by toe erosion. Two million pounds was set aside to build a new concrete toe wall to impede erosion, and to cover the costs of a beach nourishment scheme to replace material removed by longshore drift and to help dissipate wave action.

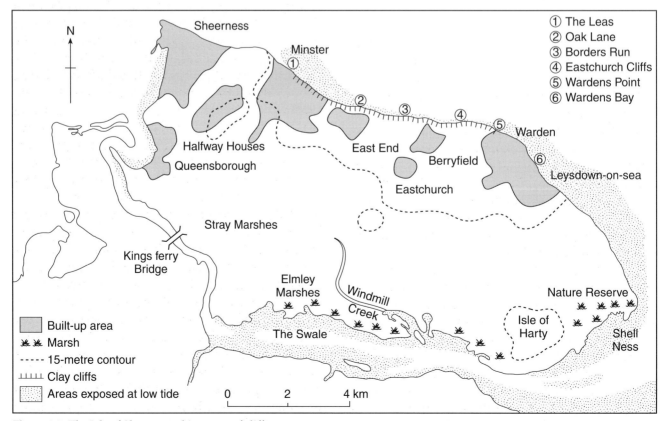

Figure 8.9 *The Isle of Sheppey and its areas of cliff retreat*

Figure 8.10 *Rip-rap and seawall defences at Reculver*

At Warden Bay, the location of Warden Springs Holiday Camp and numerous permanent residences, there is also a stretch of coastline under threat. Twenty-two old groynes and a small sea-wall, were having very little impact on erosion rates in the cliffs; the council therefore allotted a quarter of a million pounds to strengthen the old sea-wall. In the other four locations, the engineer could not justify further expenditure upon coastal defences; where there are high slumped clay cliffs, very little can be done to slow down long-term erosion and cliff recession. For example, at Boarers Run and Warden Point, Minster, the cost of proper remedial action would be prohibitive.

Along the north coast of Sheppey, therefore, the main concern has been to protect property, but it is cheaper to move caravans and other less permanent structures away from the cliff edges than to create new sea defences. As with other parts of Britain, especially with the escalating costs of engineering works, the current wisdom has been to let nature take its course along the coast, rather than continue to fight against it – a philosophy which is in line with the feelings of environmentalists.

DUNGENESS

Seen from the air, Dungeness has an elegantly sculpted cuspate form. At ground level, however, its extensive open landscape composed of numerous shingle ridges known locally as 'fulls', is interrupted by the ugly shapes of nuclear power stations, gravel extraction plants and shabby holiday homes. This unique feature, the largest cuspate foreland in Europe, contains 40 per cent of Britain's coastal shingle and is a complex structure; its formation has been the subject of much debate by geomorphologists, involving theories about coastal currents, longshore drift and sea-level changes.

The overall shape of Dungeness (seen in Figure 8.11), is due to the way in which the positions of various shingle spits have shifted as they have extended from the south towards Hythe. One of the explanations given for the overall shape of the foreland is that at this point opposing dominant currents from the English Channel and the North Sea meet. The area enclosed by the shingle fulls of Dungeness become the Denge, Walland and Romney Marshes, now mainly reclaimed and converted to rich pasture or arable land. Although the natural ridges prevent most of this lowland from flooding, at Dymchurch where the shingle has been breached by erosion, a sea-wall has had to be constructed. Further inland from the marshes is a line of old sea-cliffs, now degraded by subaerial erosion and covered in vegetation; these mark the old shoreline of a large bay into which rivers such as the Rother once drained. The Royal Military Canal, linking Hythe with Rye in Sussex, is now the main drainage feature of Dungeness and its adjacent marshes. Perched high and dry on the old sea-cliffs, villages such as Appledore and Hamstreet were once ports, but are now 10 to 15 km from the sea.

Evidence found in the shingle deposits together with some information from historical maps have enabled geomorphologists to piece together the most likely explanation of the evolution of Dungeness. Figure 8.11 shows the shifting positions of the spits over the last 3000 years, influenced in particular by the changing level of the sea. The spit started off with shingle from the eroded cliffs near Fairlight in Sussex being pushed north-eastwards by the prevailing south–westerly winds (stages 1 and 2). Eventually, the spit extended across the whole bay as far as Hythe (stage 3). A rise in sea level is likely to have led to more rapid erosion of the cliffs to the south–west of Dungeness, which in turn left the shingle more exposed to the action of the south–westerlies which

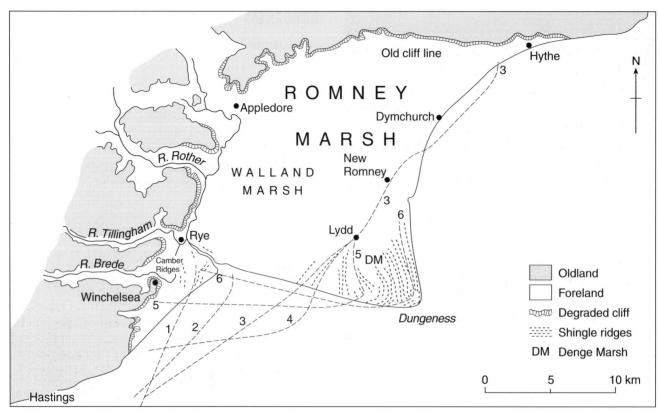

Figure 8.11 *Dungeness and its evolution*

then caused the spit to shift round to a west–east alignment because of longshore drift (stages 4 and 5 show the reorientation of the spit). Large amounts of material are deposited at the hook of the ness, where the waves from the south–west lose their energy through refraction, and are also partly shaped by the occasional east–north–east storm winds coming from the North Sea through the Straits of Dover. Today, shingle continues to be deposited on the southern shore of Dungeness, but is being eroded from the eastern shore where very little new material accumulates. Indeed, ever since the 15th century it has been necessary to build sea-walls in the Dymchurch area to protect the shingle from erosion and Romney Marsh from flooding.

COASTLINE AND CONSERVATION

As noted above, Kent has one of the most altered stretches of coastline in Britain. Built-up areas cover 50 per cent of the county's shoreline; as well as housing, power stations and heavy industry are built along the coast and dump waste products into the sea. Defences against marine erosion and transportation have been constructed along 45 per cent of the coast, even if they are frequently to little avail. Despite all this human interference, Kent has many coastal areas of great ecological and environmental importance.

Dungeness is a unique ecological zone; because of the sheer scale of its shingle deposits it has numerous rare plant species as well as being the only home in Britain of six types of butterflies and moths. Kent also has eight important wet grassland habitats, five of which, including the Swale Marshes and Romney Marsh, are Sites of Special Scientific Interest (SSSIs.) There are four important saltmarsh habitats in Kent, the most extensive of which, the Medway estuary with an area of 754 ha is one of the largest in Britain; these are all major breeding grounds for a wide range of wading birds and waterfowl.

As Kent was on the main routeway for the invasion of Britain from prehistoric times through to the Normans, its coastline also harbours some 25 historical and archaeological sites of national importance which, like the ecological sites, require special conservation status. Some of these conservation areas are under international conventions, others are designated by national conservation criteria and some are just nature reserves protected by local organisations.

SUMMARY

● A wide variety of coastal features due to geology
● The main high cliff areas correspond to the chalk
● The various clay cliffs are very unstable
● The Roman shoreline was very different from that today
● Most erosion is carried out during storm surges
● Recession rates can average 1 m per year
● Dungeness is the largest cuspate foreland in Europe and its origins are complex
● The Isle of Sheppey has several areas of dangerous cliffs but only some areas are worth protecting
● Kent has one of the country's most urbanised coasts, yet there are numerous different types of conservation area

 EXAMINATION QUESTIONS

This case study tends to lend itself just to coastal features, their origin and management, but a broader context could also be found.

SPECIFIC

Specific questions could include:

1 With reference to an area or region you have studied, account for the great variety of features which may be found along its coastline.
2 Examine the variety of factors such as wind, waves, tides and geology which influence the evolution of a stretch of coastline which you have studied.

GENERAL

More general use of the case study could be:

3 To what extent should humans protect the environment from the changes resulting from natural processes? Illustrate your answer with specific examples.
4 To what extent can coastlines be perceived to be hazardous environments?

— CASE STUDY — ⑨

THE HAZARDOUS ENVIRONMENT OF CENTRAL AMERICA

The Central American isthmus is riddled with instability. Here the meeting of north and south funnels a range of opposing forces into close contact, generating tension which manifests itself in volcanic eruptions, earthquakes and political upheaval.

Norton and Whatmore, Cadogan Guide to Central America

The seven small countries which occupy the isthmus of land between Mexico and Colombia (see Figure 9.1) have had turbulent histories due to their exposure to both tectonic and meteorological hazards. Natural disasters have held back their economic development, by destroying cities and harvests and taking lives and livelihoods, thereby leaving some of them amongst the poorest nations of the Western Hemisphere. Many of them have also been politically turbulent, with corrupt ruling families, military dictatorships and revolutions which have

given Central America the popular image of being composed of 'banana republics'. Sometimes the natural disasters and political events have been intricately intertwined – as in the case of Nicaragua in the 1970s and 1980s.

Natural disasters have hit at the political heart of most of these nations, and at various times capital cities have been destroyed and rebuilt elsewhere: Belize moved its capital from Belize City to Belmopan because of hurricanes; Costa Rica, Guatemala and El Salvador have all moved their capitals following earthquake devastation;

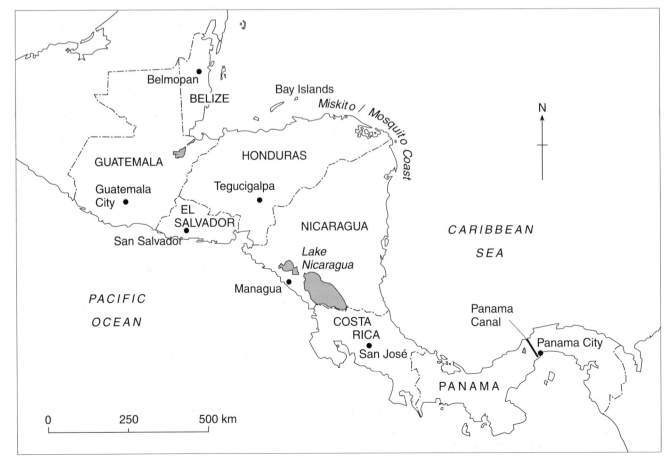

Figure 9.1 *The countries of Central America*

Managua, the capital of Nicaragua, is left with an eerily empty CBD after the quake of 1972.

STRUCTURAL AND ENVIRONMENTAL BACKGROUND

As can be seen from Figure 9.1, the three southernmost countries (Panama, Costa Rica and Nicaragua) have almost equal lengths of Caribbean and Pacific coastline; Honduras has a long Caribbean and shorter Pacific outlet in contrast to Guatemala with a long Pacific coast and a short stretch on the Caribbean. The two smallest countries, Belize and El Salvador, are located on the Caribbean and Pacific respectively. These locations are important when considering the countries' susceptibilities to natural hazards. Figure 9.2 shows how tectonic disturbances in the region are more likely to be felt towards the Pacific side (whereas hurricanes substantially affect the Caribbean coastline).

The isthmus of Central America is located at the junction of three tectonic plates, the Nazca and Cocos to the west and the Caribbean to the east. At this point along the Pacific coast there is a subduction zone where the Cocos Plate is being drawn down under the Caribbean Plate; in the process this has created the Acapulco Deep ocean trench (which reaches a maximum depth of 6652 m) and the various ranges of fold mountains and volcanoes which form the spine of Central America (the highest peak of which is Volcán de Tajumulca in Guatemala, 4210 m). Major fault lines trend through the centre of these mountains and also cut through Nicaragua and Guatemala from the Caribbean. Earthquakes, therefore, mainly occur on the western side of Central America – but not exclusively.

The tracks followed by hurricanes in the Caribbean and Central America, normally occur between the months of June and October. They result from the build-up of intense tropical depressions over the warm Atlantic waters to the south-east of the Caribbean; they then track westwards towards the Caribbean islands and the mainland of Central America, usually then turning northwards towards the Gulf Coast of the United States. Maximum damage occurs in Central America when the northwards deflection fails to occur, as in 1969 when Hurricane Francella

the hazardous environment of Central America

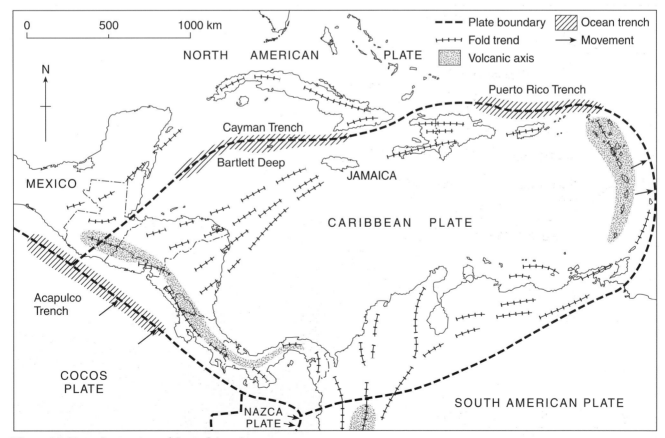

Figure 9.2 *Tectonic structure of Central America*

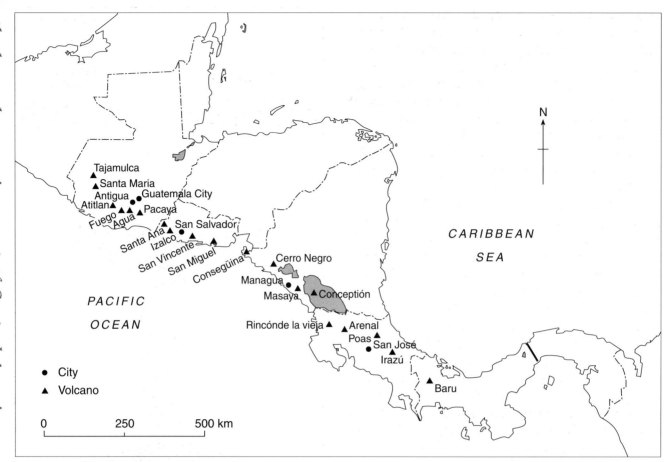

Figure 9.3 *Major volcanoes of Central America*

destroyed 90 per cent of coastal Belize's banana crop, and in 1975 when Hurricane Joan devastated the coastal town of Bluefields in Nicaragua. Of the countries with Caribbean coastlines, Belize's situation in the north makes it the most vulnerable to hurricanes, whereas Panama in the south is the least vulnerable.

VOLCANOES OF CENTRAL AMERICA

The mountainous stretch of land from western Guatemala through to western Panama is one of six well-defined areas of concentrated volcanic activity within Latin America. There are hundreds of peaks of volcanic origin and 67 recently active volcanoes, 32 of which are currently active to some degree (from continuous eruptions down to smoking fumaroles). Figure 9.3 locates some of the main Central American volcanoes.

Most of the Central American volcanoes have over 50 per cent silica content in their magma – making them either andesitic (intermediate) or rhyolitic (acidic). As these types of magma are viscose, they tend to cool quickly, block vents and therefore make the volcanoes very

volatile; thus the main materials ejected are pumice, lapilli and other forms of pyroclastic rock. These volcanoes are generally 'strato-volcanoes', with distinctive cone shapes built up from layer upon layer of ash with each eruption; however, deep underneath may be concealed the typical dome shape associated with viscose lava. Past violence has converted numerous volcanoes of the region into calderas with broad craters containing one or more lakes and fumarole activity.

When volcanoes are categorised according to the

Figure 9.4 *The volcano Agua*

nature of their eruptions, the terms used are 'Hawaiian', 'Strombolian', 'Vulcanian', 'Vesuvian' and 'Plinian', based upon an ascending order of violence (see Figure 9.5). The term 'Pelean' is used to describe eruptions accompanied by huge incandescent clouds of ash and gas (*nuées ardentes*) which tumble down the flanks of volcanoes, engulfing everything in their path.

There are no Hawaiian-type volcanoes in the region because it is on the wrong sort of plate margin and its volcanoes produce acidic rather than basic lava. However, Pacaya (2544 m), in Guatemala, is a typical 'Strombolian' volcano, erupting pyroclastic materials at regular intervals (every 10 to 20 minutes); it is a fairly safe volcano to live near and its 'fireworks' are clearly visible from Guatemala City on clear nights.

Irazú (3432 m), in the central valley of Costa Rica, is 'Vulcanian' in its eruption pattern. Its last big eruption occurred in 1963, when it ejected ash over an area of 300 km², destroying much of the local coffee crop and causing tremors in the nearby city of Cartago, the former capital of Costa Rica which had already been destroyed several times by earthquakes. The summit area of Irazú, which has two main craters, is a wilderness of ash and toxic fumes, but lower down the slopes rich volcanic soils support highly productive market gardening.

Arenal (1633 m), in northern Costa Rica, which has a perfectly formed ash cone, is 'Vesuvian' in its activity. In 1968, after a long period of quiescence, it erupted scattering volcanic bombs over a wide area, killing 64 people in neighbouring villages. Large blocks were propelled over 5 km from the crater and it has been calculated that their ejection must have been at a speed of 600 m/s. Arenal is currently still active but not in a destructive phase.

The eruption of Santa Maria volcano in Guatemala (3715 m), in 1902, was with 'Plinian' violence. The old lava dome was blown off, there were pyroclastic flows downslope and, within 20 hours, 12 k³ of pumice had erupted to form a 28 km high column in the atmosphere. An estimated 6000 people perished along with Guatemala's coffee crop.

Cosegüina (847 m), in Nicaragua, when it underwent a 'Plinian' eruption in 1835 produced the greatest explosion ever recorded in the Western Hemisphere – more violent than the famous eruption of Pelée on the island of Martinique in 1902. A caldera, with a clear blue lake in it, the volcano was regarded locally as extinct. On 20

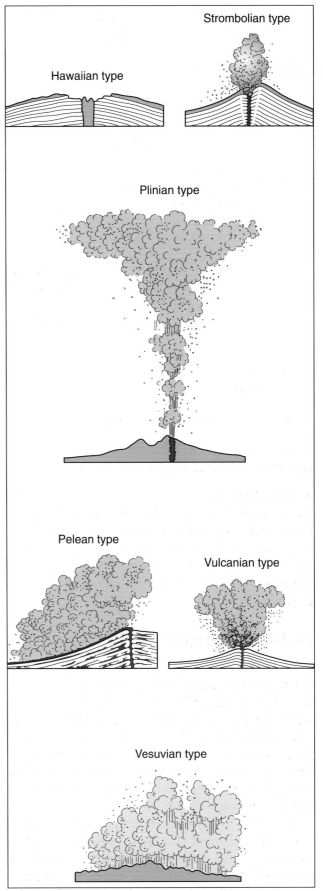

Figure 9.5 *Classification of volcanoes by eruption type*

January Caseguina let out a huge white plume of pumice into the atmosphere, which soon turned incandescent and darkness fell over a wide region. Two days later Caseguina exploded with such violence that the eruption was heard in Kingston, Jamaica, and in Bogotá, Colombia, both some 1500 km distant. Villages and farmland were buried over an area of 160 km radius of the crater, and Guatemala City remained in darkness for five days. At least 800 people living close to the volcano perished, but luckily this was not a densely populated area. 'Plinian' eruptions typically last only a few days and, being more destructive than constructive, produce gaping calderas rather than well-formed cones.

Vulcanism is not just perceived in a negative way by the people of Central America. Some of the richest farmlands are in volcanic areas (e.g. Costa Rica's and Guatemala's main coffee growing regions are located on the fertile soils of their volcanic highlands). Geothermal power has great potential in many parts of Central America, but as yet is still in its early stages of development; power stations include that at Momotombito in Central Nicaragua.

EARTHQUAKES IN CENTRAL AMERICA

Much more dramatic and damaging than volcanic activity have been a series of earthquakes which have struck at major centres of population in the region. Many of the main cities of Central America are located close to fault lines within mountain basins which are surrounded by the brooding forms of quiescent volcanoes. Antigua, the former capital of Guatemala founded by the Spanish in 1547, has been flattened by earthquakes on several occasions; its coat of arms shows the three volcanic peaks which rise above the city, symbols of the area's tectonic instability. In 1773, Antigua was so badly damaged that the capital was moved 50 km away to what is now Guatemala City. However, in 1976 Guatemala City was itself victim of a massive earthquake, which yet again undermined the historic urban fabric of Antigua.

Similar events have affected the central valley of Costa Rica. Cartago was the original capital of the Spanish colony, but located in an area of great instability; in 1723, it was destroyed by an eruption of the volcano Irazú and the capital was moved to San José in 1821. Since then, Cartago was twice hit by violent earthquakes, in 1841 and 1910. San José is much less vulnerable than the old capital, but is not totally immune from earthquake damage.

MANAGUA EARTHQUAKE OF 1972

Central Nicaragua is a high disturbed zone of tectonic activity. Surrounded by volcanoes and crater lakes (see Figure 9.7), Managua was victim of severe earthquakes in both 1931 and 1972, the effects of the latter being still clearly visible more than 25 years later. The results of tectonic instability in 1972 were eventually to lead to civil strife and the overthrow of the Somoza regime by the revolutionary Sandinistas.

Managua was established as a compromise capital in the 19th century because of the rival claims of the country's two most important cities, the intellectual and liberal university city of Léon to the north and the conservative commercial port city of Grenada to the south. It had already suffered at least nine earthquakes which caused structural damage before the devastation of 1931, but the 1972 earthquake was worse still.

On 23 December when the people of Managua were preparing for Christmas, an earthquake measuring 6.5 on the Richter Scale rocked the city, destroying most of its centre and parts of the suburbs. Around 10 000 people were killed, 20 000 injured and 50 000 made homeless. In the CBD some 36 blocks of the city's colonial grid pattern were flattened, leaving just a few buildings such as the cathedral standing as

Figure 9.6 *Earthquake memorial in Managua*

ruins. The estimated population of Managua in December 1972 had been around 410 000; within a few weeks it had dropped to just 170 000 as people fled to other parts of the country in fear of further destruction or to live with relatives.

The Somoza family, who owned great swathes of the nation's wealth and had ruled Nicaragua with a rod of iron since they came to power following a military coup in 1935, set up a National Emergency Committee to deal with the earthquake relief. Top priority was given to rebuilding middle-class residential suburbs, although some foreign aid did help to establish temporary homes for the poor (e.g. US funding built 11 000 housing units). However, the reconstruction of the CBD was forbidden. There was widespread corruption as emergency supplies were sold off for profit by the regime's National Guard and most of the rebuilding contracts involved the Somoza family because they owned the country's biggest cement company.

Corruption, poverty, high inflation and general dissatisfaction led to the deterioration of the country into civil war, with guerrilla warfare against the regime and many brutal murders of its political opponents. The opposition FSLN or Sandinistas gained more and more ground in the country until they eventually took over in 1979. The earthquake had killed 10 000, but the civil war it had sparked off killed some 50 000, injured 100 000, made over 150 000 homeless and caused another 150 000 to leave Nicaragua altogether.

Managua's CBD, despite a plan of 1982, has still not been reconstructed but remains a mixture of ruined buildings covered in political graffiti, a few squatter houses, land which has been grassed over and isolated monuments such as that to the 1931 and 1972 earthquakes. Today, with a population of well over 1 million, the suburbs sprawl in all directions; there are, however, sharp distinctions between the rich and poor districts. CBD functions have been devolved to the smarter residential suburbs with their *centros comerciales* or US-style shopping malls, which tend to be located on the main highways out of town. The poorer, high-density, post-earthquake housing is concentrated mainly in the east of the city, where the new general market was established to replace that destroyed in 1972.

The social polarisation of housing in the city, which already existed prior to 1972, has merely

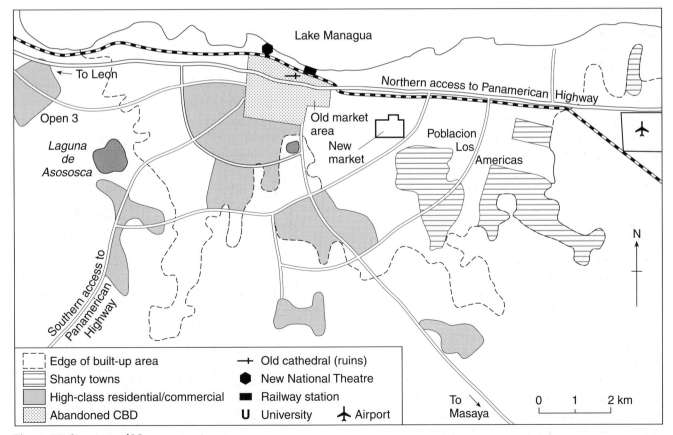

Figure 9.7 *Structure of Managua*

the hazardous environment of Central America

Figure 9.8 *Earthquake monitoring stations*

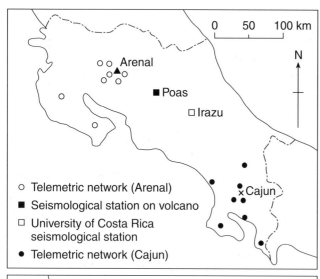

○ Telemetric network (Arenal)
■ Seismological station on volcano
□ University of Costa Rica
   seismological station
● Telemetric network (Cajun)

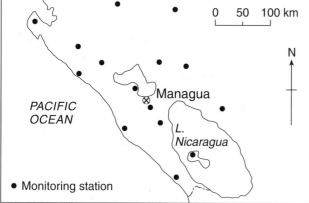

● Monitoring station

a *Costa Rica*   b *Nicaragua*

become more extreme since the earthquake, despite all the reforms introduced by the Marxist Sandinistas during their ten and a half years of government. One of the main causes of Nicaragua's poverty which gave the astonishing inflation rate of 36 000 per cent in 1988, was the deliberate policy of the United States to destroy the Sandinista regime.

GUATEMALA EARTHQUAKE OF 1976

The earthquake which befell the region around Guatemala City was more destructive than that which destroyed Managua four years earlier. Guatemala City is close to the Motagua Valley faultline, part of the junction between the North American and Caribbean tectonic plates, which runs for 300 km east to west through Guatemala. The 'quake which took place on 4 February at 3 a.m., when most people were in bed, measured 7.5 on the Richter Scale and claimed over 23 000 lives, leaving a further 77 000 homeless. The displacement of the ground at the epicentre on the day of the earthquake was 1.3 m, compared to the average rate of movement along the Montagua Valley of 2 m per 100 years.

The high death toll was explained both by the time of the earthquake and by the nature of much of the housing in the city and surrounding area. In 1975 Guatemala had a shortage of some 675 000 houses, and the earthquake in 1976 merely increased this by another 250 000. Hundreds of thousands of the urban poor live in shanty towns on the western outskirts of the city; their squatter suburbs being located on the edges of ravines carved in the volcanic tuffs deposited by past eruptions of Pacaya and other volcanoes. The houses are generally made of flimsy adobe with no resistance to earth tremors and, during the night of 4 February 1976, were battered by the double onslaught of the earthquake itself and the numerous landslides which it triggered. An estimated 30 per cent of all the adobe buildings in the immediate vicinity of the city were destroyed and those inhabitants left without homes numbered more than 1 million. The old capital of Antigua, 50 km to the west, was once again severely damaged in the 1976 earthquake, just as it had been by similar events in 1586, 1717, 1773, 1874 and 1917. Today, most of its houses have been rebuilt, but dozens of Spanish colonial churches lie in ruins.

The earthquake relief in Guatemala was much more efficient and less corrupt than in Nicaragua, but in the long run caused similar political disruption. The damage caused by the disaster was over US $ 75 million, or 20 per cent of the country's GDP. The CRN, *Comite de Reconstuccion Nacional* (Committee for National Reconstruction) administered the emergency aid efficiently, but reconstruction was slow and as hundreds of thousands of people were dislocated by the earthquake, civil unrest grew. The trade unions fought for better social conditions, a guerrilla army took to the hills to fight for the people's rights and an anti-Communist secret army waged war against them. For more than 20 years an undercover brutal struggle between these armed factions disrupted life in Guatemala and showed signs of being resolved only in the late 1990s.

EARTHQUAKE MONITORING

Despite experiencing so much tectonic activity, the countries of Central America have been slow to develop earthquake and volcanic monitoring stations because of their limited financial resources. Figure 9.8 shows the monitoring station networks

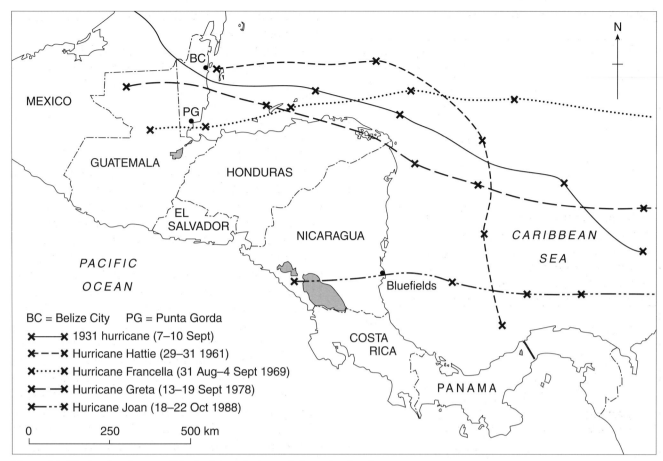

Figure 9.9 *The tracks of some of Central America's most damaging hurricanes*

for **a** Costa Rica and **b** Nicaragua. Since 1970, Costa Rica has studied its tectonic activity with various seismological networks. The main concerns are to watch activity in the central valley where most of the fault lines are located, to monitor its volcanoes, especially Poas and Irazú and to check the stability of areas where two major hydroelectric dams are planned at Cajón in the south and Arenal in the north. Nicaragua has just one national seismological monitoring network. Its main areas of close study are the Masaya and Managua areas, as well as the other volcanoes and two proposed hydroelectric sites at Mojolta and Copalar.

HURRICANES IN CENTRAL AMERICA

In contrast to the tectonic hazards of the Pacific side of Central America, the Caribbean coast is prone to hurricanes. Figure 9.9 shows the tracks of some of the most destructive hurricanes to hit the region during the 20th century. Some parts of the Caribbean coast are more likely to be hit than others, and much depends on the orientation of the coastline. Belize and Nicaragua have coastlines at right angles to the pathways of oncoming storms, whereas the northern part of the Honduras coast

runs parallel to them and is subject to fewer hurricanes, although the Bay Islands are not immune to the destructive effects of tropical storms.

The general tendency for these hurricanes of Atlantic origin is to move westwards through the centre of the Caribbean, then suddenly change direction to a more northerly route towards the Gulf Coast of the United States; when the change of direction fails to take place, Belize, Nicaragua and Honduras often suffer intense damage.

BELIZE AND ITS HURRICANES

Belize City is in a vulnerable position for advancing hurricanes; it has been almost totally destroyed on three occasions: 1787, 1931 and 1961. The 1931 hurricane is well documented in the book *Cyclone!* by Ernest Cain, written as a report for the colonial administration of what was then British Honduras. The hurricane struck as people were preparing to celebrate the colony's birthday on 10 September, so Belize City was festooned with flags and bunting. The sequence of events were as follows:

● On 8 September a warning of a moderate storm to the south of Kingston, Jamaica, was received.

the hazardous environment of Central America

- At 10:45 p.m. on 9 September a warning was received from New Orleans that the storm would pass close to Belize City.
- At 8:20 a.m. on 10 September ships were fleeing into harbours along the Honduran coast.
- At 9:30 a.m. a 56 k per hour wind was recorded by the weather station in Belize City.
- By 12:40 p.m. it measured 80 km per hour and by 1:15 p.m. 100 km per hour.
- After a lull between 1:45 and 2:00 p.m., it reached 120 km per hour and increased to 192 km per hour by 2:35 p.m.
- Between 2:50 and 3:00 p.m. it held a maximum speed of 215 km per hour, soon after which the anemometer blew away.

The wind was not the most damaging part of the environmental onslaught, but it was accompanied by a 5 m tidal wave which engulfed most of the buildings in the city and was the main reason for the loss of more than 150 lives. Material damage amounted to more than US $ 5 million and included the complete destruction of the three-storey concrete St John's College, the biggest building in the colony, together with severe damage to all the main churches and public buildings.

There was a repeat performance of these events 30 years later. On 31 October 1961, Hurricane Hattie tore its way through Belize City. It reached a maximum force of 255 km per hour and was accompanied by a 4.5 m tidal wave; 70 per cent of the city was razed and 275 people lost their lives from collapsing buildings or by drowning. When the storm abated, the whole city was a mass of tangled debris from what had been buildings, boats and cars. This amounted to more than US $ 25 million worth of damage. Hurricane Hattie also badly damaged other coastal towns in Belize, including Stann Creek and Punta Gorda. Following

Figure 9.10 *Church ruined in the 1976 Guatemala earthquake*

the wrath of Hurricane Hattie, the Belize government decided to move its capital to a site 80 km inland, to a place less vulnerable than the coast. Belmopan was founded in 1965 and began to function as the capital in 1970. Funded mainly from the British Overseas Development aid programme, its buildings are designed to withstand winds of up to 230 km per hour.

More recent hurricanes have caused serious agricultural damage; in 1969, Hurricane Francella destroyed 85 per cent of the banana crop in Belize's coastal plantations. In 1978, Hurricane Greta caused serious flooding and crop destruction, but there was no loss of life.

Hurricane Joan, in 1988, was too far south to hit Belize, but struck the Mosquito Coast of Nicaragua, leaving Bluefields, the principal port city with a population of 60 000, 90 per cent destroyed. The wind, which had reached 230 km per hour, killed 360 people in Nicaragua and wiped out 70 per cent of the country's fishing fleet as well as destroying the work in progress on the new deep-water port for Bluefields. Unlike the Managua earthquake in 1971, no emergency aid was forthcoming from Washington, because the Sandinista regime was in power and it was regarded as an enemy of the United States.

HURRICANE MITCH

Central America came into the international headlines again, after a decade of relative obscurity, in late October 1998 when Hurricane Mitch struck Honduras and Nicaragua. The hurricane caused torrential rain which triggered off huge landslides, such as those on the slopes of Volcan Casitas, which killed some 1,500 Nicaraguans. A large number of villages in both countries were engulfed and swept away by the ensuing debris. In some of the poorer districts of Tegucigulpa located on unstable hillsides just over the other side of the Rio Choluteca from the Honduran capital's CBD, hundreds of flimsily-built shanty town shacks were washed away into the swollen river. The total number of fatalities from Hurricane Mitch is estimated at 7,000.

The disaster of autumn 1998 highlighted not only the problems of bringing emergency relief to remote regions where the infrastructure had been badly damaged, but also brought attention to the fact that MEDCs were administering aid to impoverished nations whom they had helped to land in debt, partly through unfair trade and the operations of TNCs. This led to a debate within the G7 countries on the whole theme of debt cancellation.

SUMMARY

- Seven environmentally unstable countries
- Pacific coast tectonically unstable
- Caribbean coast subject to hurricanes
- 67 active volcanoes
- Mainly acidic volcanoes, therefore volatile
- Volcanoes representing most styles of eruption
- Cosegüina, the greatest eruption of Western Hemisphere

- Managua earthquake 1972, 6.5 Richter
- Managua still has empty CBD
- Guatemala earthquake 1976, 7.5 Richter: 650 000 houses destroyed
- Belize most frequently hit by hurricanes
- Hattie 1961; Francella 1969; Greta 1978; Joan 1988; Mitch 1998

EXAMINATION QUESTIONS

This case study is hazard based, but may have wider application in terms of the economic and urban content.

SPECIFIC

Direct questions using the case study could include:

1 With reference to an area or areas you have studied, explain the causes and consequences of any natural hazards it experiences.
2 Why are some parts of the world more prone to natural hazards than others? Illustrate your answer with specific examples.

GENERAL

The wider application of the case study could include:

3 With reference to specific examples, outline the reasons for poverty and underdevelopment in LEDCs.
4 With reference to one or more urban area you have studied, examine the processes which have determined its structure.

─ CASE STUDY ─ ⑩ ─── DEMOGRAPHIC PATTERNS IN PERU

We don't want a country populated by children who search for their food amongst the rubbish tips ...

President Alberto Fujimori, 1991

The strong words, above, came from the Peruvian President when he was addressing the foreign press corps on the issue of his country's slowness in initiating a comprehensive family planning strategy. It underlines one of the key problems in LEDCs – that of rapid population growth.

Peru has a current population of 24 million, which is expected to double in the next 33 years. Although this is fairly typical of poorer LEDCs, Peru, like its Latin American neighbours, is undergoing rapid demographic change: birth rates are declining, life expectancy is increasing and rapid urbanisation is taking place.

Many aspects of Peru's population geography vary greatly from region to region – this reflects the physical divisions of the country as well as its history and ethnic structure. The country is divided into 24 departments (see Figure 10.1) for which detailed statistics are available, helping to illustrate these strong regional contrasts.

PHYSICAL ENVIRONMENT

Peru can be divided into three distinct physical regions. Along the Pacific Coast, varying in width from 50 to 150 km, is the Peruvian desert, an extension of the Chilean Atacama. With few perennial rivers, it is one of the driest places in the world and comprises only 11 per cent of Peru's territory. Beyond the desert rise the Cordilleras of the Andes which, accounting for a further 31 per cent of

Figure 10.1 *Peruvian departments*

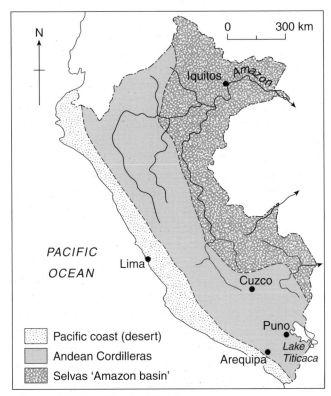

Figure 10.2 *Peru: Physical divisions*

Peruvian territory, are dominated by three main north-west to south-east trending ridges and some 50 peaks over 6000 m. Within the Cordilleras are numerous intermontane basins, including that occupied by Lake Titicaca, at 3809 m the highest major lake in the world. To the north and east of the Andes is an area of rainforest-clad lowlands, drained by the meandering head tributaries of the Amazon, the least developed part of Peru, despite the fact that it covers 58 per cent of the country's land area (see Figure 10.2a).

POPULATION DISTRIBUTION

Figures 10.3 and 10.4 show the population densities of the 24 Peruvian departments. The densities vary from 0.8 people per km² in the forest department of Madre di Dios to 203.5 per km² in Lima, the capital. From the map, it can be seen clearly that the coastal plain area is the most densely populated zone of Peru, the equatorial rainforest the least populated, and the Sierras fall somewhere in between. This is more a reflection of the way in which Peru was colonised than the economic potentials of the three natural regions.

The coastal plain was the main focus of Spanish settlement from the 16th century onwards. Lima, Tumbes, Tacna, Trujillo and the other cities of the coastal plain have acted as 'magnets' to migrants from rural areas. At the same time, as agricultural methods including irrigation have improved, some of the rural desert areas have encouraged migrants from other parts of the country. The coastal plain also has a number of important mining settlements.

The less densely populated departments of the Sierras, especially in the south-east, are those with the biggest concentrations of Pre-Colombian Indians, the descendants of the Incas. These departments are in economic decline and, as they have high birth rates, they also experience considerable emigration.

The sparsely populated forest departments are Peru's 'New Frontier'. The discovery of oil and other minerals in the Amazon region, together with the resources of the forests themselves, are encouraging economic development and, therefore, immigration from other parts of Peru. The changing fortunes of Peru's three main natural regions can be seen in Figure 10.2b. Particularly notable are the decline of the Andean region since the 1940s (from 64 per cent of the population in 1940 to 30 per cent today), the rapid economic growth of the coastal plain (with its population rising from 30 per cent to 61 per cent) and the more recent rapid growth in importance of the forested lowlands.

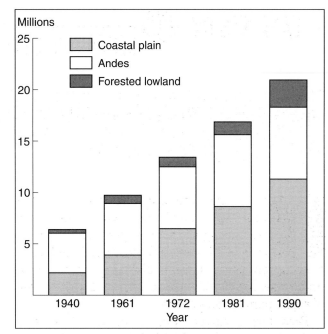

Figure 10.3 *Peru's changing population by physical region*

HISTORICAL BACKGROUND

The current population distribution of Peru must be seen in the context of the historical past. Advanced cultures evolved along the Pacific some 3000 years ago, but the Andes offered a more favourable environment for settlement and agriculture than either the desert or the rainforest. In the valleys of the Cordilleras, the Pre-Colombian Indians

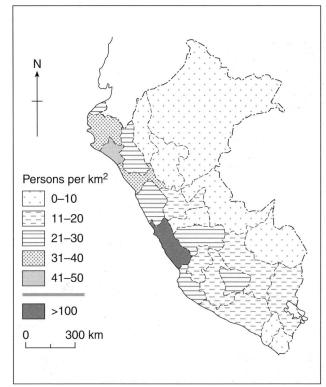

Figure 10.4 *Peru: Population density*

developed the complex social structure that gave rise to the Inca civilisation. From its capital in Cuzco, by the late 15th century the Inca Empire controlled present-day Peru, Bolivia, Ecuador and northern parts of Chile and Argentina.

When the Spanish conquistadores arrived in the early 16th century, what is now south-east Peru was the most densely populated part of South America. Once the Spanish founded Lima and other cities near the Pacific, the population balance started to shift away from the Andes towards the coastal plain. However, it is only with the heavy urbanisation of the last few decades that the coastal plain has become so predominant in the Peruvian economy.

Figure 10.5 *An Andean market showing people of Inca origin in traditional costume*

POPULATION DYNAMICS

In 1900, Peru had a population of just 3.8 millions, but since then it has grown more than six-fold. Rates of growth have not been constant during the 20th century; in 1900, growth rates were around 1 per cent per annum, increasing to 1.5 per cent by 1920. The total population remained relatively small as death rates were almost as high as birth rates – Peru had not yet begun to undergo demographic transition.

By 1950, death rates had declined to just 23 per thousand, whereas birth rates remained high, at 48 per thousand. The main reason for these changes was improved medicine and, in particular, the reduction of infant mortality through vaccinations and better health care. In the 1950s Peru had, therefore, entered the 'early expanding stage' of demographic transition.

Growth rates peaked between 1960 and 1965, when they reached 2.9 per cent per annum, as can be seen in Figure 10.6. This was due to birth rates remaining high for social and economic reasons,

while death rates were already in decline. Since 1965, growth rates have also been in continuous decline. At present, the population growth rate is 2.1 per cent per annum and it is predicted to decline below 2 per cent by the year 2000, and eventually to as little as 0.1 per cent – the typical European level – by 2025.

Year	Rates per thousand	
	Births	**Deaths**
1950	48	23
1960	44	19
1970	41	15
1980	37	12
1990	33	9
2000	24	7

Figure 10.6 *Peru's birth and death rates since 1950*

Birth rates have been in sharp decline since 1950, but the rate of decline has been more pronounced since 1985. Reasons for this – and Peru's entry into the

Figure 10.7 *Spanish colonial buildings in Cuzco*

'late expanding stage' of demographic transition – include a wider application of family planning, a better status for women, improved education and a decline in infant mortality. The government's perception is, nevertheless, that the country's population is still growing too rapidly.

Birth rates vary greatly from one department to another, the highest being 38 per thousand in Huancavelica, a rural mountain area, and the lowest in metropolitan Lima, at 23 per thousand. Figure 10.5 shows the more urbanised coastal plain to have lower than average birth rates.

Death rates similarly vary from one part of Peru to another, with Huancavalica the highest at 16 per thousand and Lima the lowest at 5 per thousand. Two important factors need to be considered here:

- hospitals and medical facilities are more concentrated in the capital
- the more rural departments are left with an ageing population because of the emigration of the young.

There are also big regional variations in infant mortality (see Figure 10.9).

Another result of changes in birth and death rates has been the dramatic improvement in life expectancy, from the mid 40s in 1950 to 64 for men and 68 for women in 1995 (see Figure 10.10). There are also huge differences in life expectancy between departments, with the rural areas of the southern Sierras such as that around Cuzco having the lowest life expectancy (between 50 and 55 years), and the urbanised coastal departments such as Lima having the highest (over 70 years). Again, this illustrates the medical and welfare advantages of modern city life over those in the more remote rural areas.

CONTROLLING BIRTHS

In the 1960s, when Peru was under a military dictatorship, all foreign-sponsored family planning organisations were shut down as they were deemed to be 'imperialist' (i.e. foreign interference in Peruvian affairs). The present government acknowledges that the country's population is growing too rapidly, but there has never been a national campaign to suggest ideal family size, as in India, Indonesia or Tunisia. Family planning is recognised as a part of the whole health education issue and throughout the country information is available at hospitals and clinics.

THE INFLUENCE OF THE CHURCH

There is least action on family planning in the more remote rural areas where illiteracy and poverty levels are high, yet these are the areas where it is most needed. It is estimated that 48 per cent of

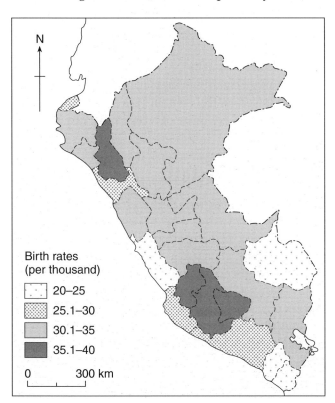

Figure 10.8 *Peru: Regional variations in birth rates*

Birth rates
(per thousand)

- 20–25
- 25.1–30
- 30.1–35
- 35.1–40

0   300 km

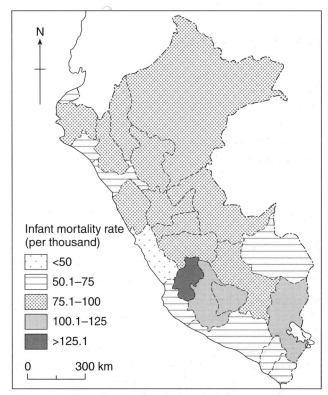

Figure 10.9 *Peru: Regional variations in infant mortality*

Infant mortality rate
(per thousand)

- <50
- 50.1–75
- 75.1–100
- 100.1–125
- >125.1

0   300 km

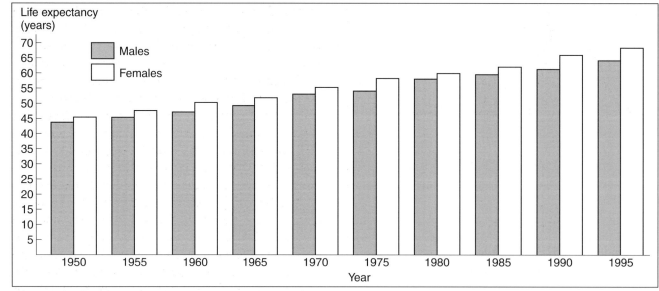

Figure 10.10 *Peru: Changing life expectancy*

married Peruvian women use some form of contraceptive device, but 39 per cent of couples still rely on the rhythm method advocated by the Roman Catholic Church.

Ninety per cent of Peruvians are nominally Roman Catholics, therefore the Church has a strong influence over the people. The Catholic hierarchy has come into conflict with the government over family planning. In 1991, the Peruvian President Fujimori put into action a new scheme to make free information on family planning more widely available; it was supported by 1.2 million dollars from the United Nations. At the same time the Cardinal Archbishop Vergas Alzamora of Lima was preaching from his pulpit that the Church condemned all forms of artificial contraception and that women who used them '*no ir al ciel*' (will not go to heaven).

The Church is strongest in the poorer rural areas where many people would genuinely live in fear of disobeying the Catholic teaching.

THE HEALTH OF THE NATION

Although the health of the average Peruvian is improving, the country still has the second highest infant mortality rate in South America (75 per thousand to Bolivia's 78 per thousand). This appears to be a problem associated with the more remote rural areas of the Andes. Three major causes account for 71 per cent of children's deaths in Peru: respiratory infections, diarrhoeal diseases and complications associated with birth. All three are a great problem in the rural Andes environment, with

high altitudes, lack of piped water and sewage, and poor medical facilities.

Peru suffers from endemic diseases which have been wiped out elsewhere. The plague has been endemic since 1903. In 1992 an outbreak led to some 1000 cases and 54 deaths. Modern vaccination programmes limited the spread of the plague. Far worse was the cholera epidemic of 1991–2, with more than 500 000 cases and some 3000 fatalities. Even so, a nationwide information campaign as well as vaccinations again kept the size of the epidemic well below what it would have been 50 years ago.

The population of Lima is potentially much healthier than those living elsewhere in Peru. Of the 174 000 physicians working in the country, 60 per cent are based in the capital. It is a myth that large cities in LEDCs are more of a health hazard than the countryside.

POPULATION STRUCTURE

Changing population dynamics result in a changing population structure. The lowering of birth rates and increased life expectancy have led to a new balance of age structures. Figure 10.11 shows how the age groups are changing over a 20-year period. The changes may be gradual, but they are significant. The percentage of the population under 14 (and therefore, in theory, not of working age), is declining by 4 per cent per decade. At the same time, the population over 65 years of age is slowly increasing – at a rate of 0.5 per cent per decade. This means that Peru's dependency ratio is becoming more favourable, with over 60 per cent of the people

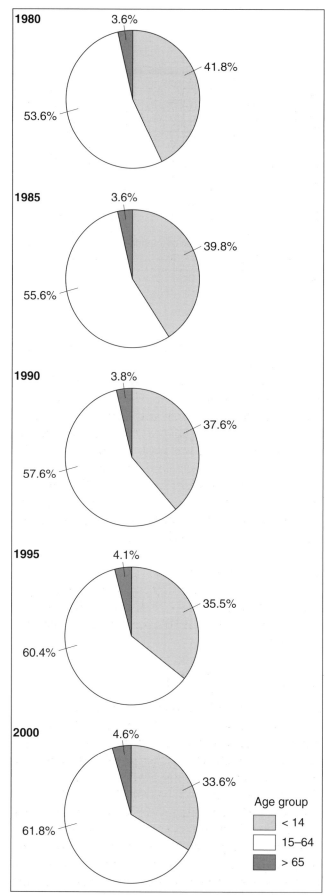

Figure 10.11 *Peru: Balance of age groups*

1980
3.6%
41.8%
53.6%

1985
3.6%
39.8%
55.6%

1990
3.8%
37.6%
57.6%

1995
4.1%
35.5%
60.4%

2000
4.6%
33.6%
61.8%

Age group
< 14
15–64
> 65

of working age in 1995. By the year 2025, given a projected population growth rate of just 0.1 per cent per annum, Peru will have an unfavourable dependency ratio as a result of an ageing population.

Figure 10.12 shows the overall effects of changing population dynamics on Peru's age structure. The population pyramid for 1965 was typical of a rapidly expanding population, whereas that of 1990 reveals the growth rate in decline. No longer is Peru so heavily weighted towards young children.

Peru has a multi-ethnic population. Forty-five per cent of the people are of Pre-Colombian Indian stock and include the descendants of the Incas and the various tribes of Amazon Indians. Only 15 per cent are of pure Spanish blood, but 37 per cent are *Mestizos* (i.e. of mixed Spanish and Indian descent). The remaining 3 per cent are from a variety of backgrounds, including Japanese migrants who came to Peru during the economic depression in rural Japan in the 1880s.

Figure 10.13 shows the regional balance of spoken Spanish and Quechua (the main Pre-Colombian Indian language). The departments of the former Inca heartlands of south-east Peru, not surprisingly, have the biggest concentrations of Quechua speakers. By contrast, the coastal, more urbanised departments and the lands of the Amazon lowlands are much more strongly Spanish speaking.

URBANISATION AND OTHER TYPES OF MIGRATION

Peru has been subject to a series of complex migration patterns, some of which are continuing today. Figure 10.14 is a model which summarises these patterns. When the Spanish arrived, they added a new layer of settlement to the existing Inca one. This involved much greater colonisation of the coastal plain. Since then there has been a continuous flow of population from the Sierras towards the Pacific Coast. The Andes are still losing population today.

Rural–urban migration has been the most significant form of migration in the last 50 years. The 'push' factors of rural poverty and the 'pull' factors of the opportunities offered by urban life are the reasons for this migration. The present degree of urbanisation in the majority of Peruvian departments is at least double what it was 30 years ago. There is, once again, a clear contrast between the region of the high Andes in the south-east and the coastal plain. Departments with a low degree of urbanisation include Apurimac (26 per cent),

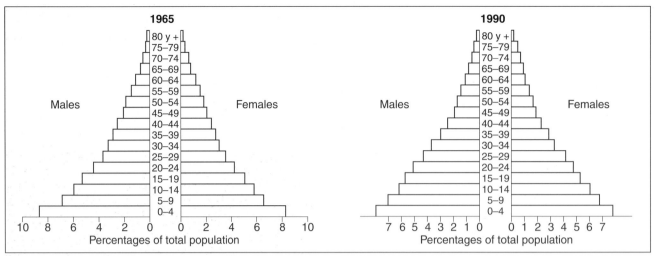

Figure 10.12 *Changing population structure 1965–90*

Huancavelica (29 per cent) and Puno (31 per cent), whereas there is a much higher degree of urbanisation in the departments of Arequipa (83 per cent), Tacna (86 per cent) and Lima (97 per cent).

The process of urbanisation has indeed been most extreme in the metropolitan area of Lima. In 1995, Lima's population reached the 7 million mark. In 1950, Lima had just 1.1 million people, by 1985 its population had reached 5.6 million and estimates suggest it will reach 10 million in the first decade of the 21st century.

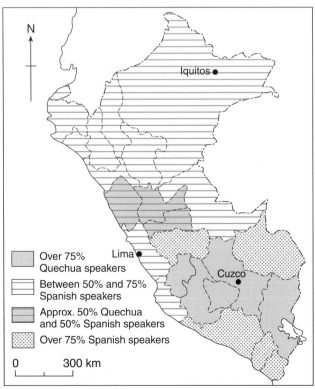

Figure 10.13 *Peru: Proportions of Spanish and Quechua speakers*

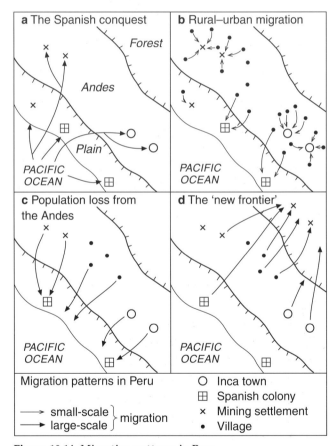

Figure 10.14 *Migration patterns in Peru*

Figure 10.15 shows the sources of migrants to Lima. It can be seen quite clearly that the largest numbers of migrants come from the more accessible departments closer to Lima, illustrating one of Ravenstein's laws of migration. With such heavy immigration, Lima has some of the worst urban problems in Latin America, its hostile desert environment merely exasperating the difficulties faced by shanty-town dwellers.

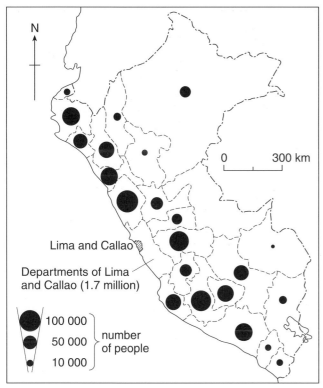

Figure 10.15 *Birthplace of people living in Lima, by region*

The other important migration process in Peru, which is still gaining momentum, is the movement of people to the 'new frontier' of Amazonia. Sparsely populated but abundant in natural resources, there is likely to be a big shift in population, especially from the Sierras, in the 21st century

Figure 10.16 *Shanty-town houses on the desert fringe of Lima*

SUMMARY

- **Population: 24 million**
- **Doubling time: 33 years**
- **Birth rate: 29 per thousand**
- **Death rate: 8 per thousand**
- **Growth rate: 2.1 per cent**
- **Life expectancy: 64 (men), 68 (women)**
- **Infant mortality: 75 per thousand**
- **Nominal RC population: 98 per cent**
- **Doctors in capital city: 60 per cent**
- **Area: 11 per cent desert; 31 per cent mountain; 58 per cent forest**
- **Departments with 'good' demographic conditions: Lima, Tacna, Lambayque**
- **Departments with 'poor' demographic conditions: Cuzco, Puno, Apurimac**

demographic patterns in Peru

EXAMINATION
QUESTIONS

Questions on population may take a wide variety of forms; they may centre on population distribution, growth, structure or movement (migration) – or combinations of two or more of these factors. They may also revolve around relationships between population and the environment, bringing in the issue of resources. Demography questions also frequently require contrasts between LEDCs and MEDCs – these would require the Peru information to be studied alongside another appropriate contrasting case study.

Population also has a bearing upon urbanisation, general development issues and the economic relationships between MEDCs and LEDCs.

In all these cases it is necessary to have as many statistics as possible to back up the answers and their key arguments. These need to cover all the main aspects of Peru's population characteristics. Also visual material selected from the maps and graphs is essential for a high-grade answer.

SPECIFIC

Examples of specific questions connected with the 'Population' topic:

1 With reference to a country or countries you have studied, describe and suggest reasons for the main changes in population distribution and density which have taken place over the last thirty years.
2 Explain to what extent regional variations in demographic patterns are the result of regional differences in the physical environment.

GENERAL

More general use of this case study, in combination with others, could help to answer such questions as:

3 Discuss the contention that high population growth is the single most important factor which holds back the economic development of LEDCs.
4 Explain why urbanisation is the dominant migration process in LEDCs, while counterurbanisation is a dominant force in MEDCs.

— CASE STUDY — 11 THE URBAN PROBLEMS OF ROME

Located in the Centre of the country, Rome combines the dynamism of the North with the grave crises of the South.

Francesco Rutelli, Mayor of Rome, 1997

Rome is, at the same time, one of the world's most beautiful cities and one of the most chaotic. Any place with such a large concentration of ancient monuments and historic buildings will have difficulty adapting to the demands of modern living but, in the case of Rome, the problems are compounded by the rapid urbanisation of recent decades together with inefficient administration interwoven with political corruption.

GEOGRAPHICAL AND HISTORICAL BACKGROUND

Rome is located in Central Italy on the flood plain of the River Tiber, 26 km from where it flows into the Tyrrhenian Sea. (See Figure 11.1.) To the east of the city are the steep slopes of the Apennine Mountains, the source of the River Aniene, the Tiber's main Roman tributary. To the north-west and the south-east of the city are volcanic calderas – reminders that

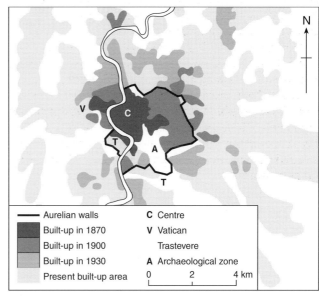

Figure 11.2 *The growth of Rome*

the region is geologically youthful and tectonically unstable. The Roman *Campagna* (the countryside around Rome), is formed mainly from thick deposits of volcanic tuffs; dissected by fluvial erosion into spurs and gorges, they provide naturally defensive sites for hundreds of historic towns and villages.

Rome itself was settled some 2750 years ago on seven of these volcanic hills, close to a convenient bridging point across the River Tiber. At the height of its Imperial power, the city of Rome had an estimated population of between 500 000 and 1 million, and its area was defined by the Aurelian Walls, constructed in AD 275 and still almost intact today (see Figure 11.2). Within these walls is the *centro storico* (historic centre), a jumble of ancient monuments, mediaeval streets, and fine Baroque palaces, squares and churches. Parts of the centre were replanned by powerful Popes who carved straight new streets through the urban fabric in the 16th and 17th centuries; again, in the 20th century, some wide avenues were constructed, but no one could have predicted the onslaught of modern motor traffic.

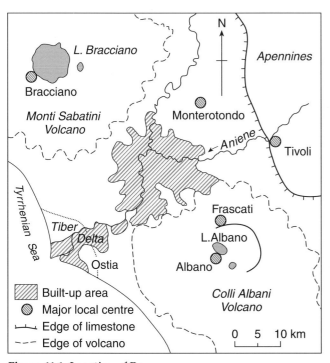

Figure 11.1 *Location of Rome*

the urban problems of Rome

Rome in the 20th century saw unprecedented population growth (see Figure 11.3). Now the municipality of 1507 km² sprawls way beyond its historical limits and only 4 per cent of the population lives within the Aurelian Walls. Throughout the 1950s, 1960s and 1970s there was heavy immigration from neighbouring rural areas as well as from the poorer regions of the Italian south, stimulating a boom in speculative housing developments which ate up large tracts of the *Campagna*. Today, with a population of 2.79 million and 2 million motor vehicles, Rome appears to be in a constant state of crisis.

Year	Population (in millions)
1880	0.2
1900	0.45
1920	0.75
1940	1.4
1960	2
1980	2.8
1990	2.79

Figure 11.3 *Rome's population growth*

TRAFFIC CONGESTION

The mediaeval street pattern of the *centro storico* is typified by narrow, winding streets, small *piazze* (squares) and alleyways. Never intended for modern traffic, they frequently become congested during working hours. Most of the city's commercial and administrative functions are concentrated in the centre and there is a daily influx of almost half a million cars. The radial road network merely funnels traffic towards the centre; the city has few circular routes connecting the radials – the road around the Aurelian Walls acts as a poor substitute for an inner ring road and is frequently jammed at peak times. Similarly, the theoretically fast-moving one-way system along the banks of the River Tiber (*Lungotevere*) is often forced into a gridlock during rush hours.

Not only is there a problem with through traffic in the city centre, but also a chronic shortage of parking areas; most parking is on-street, which merely adds to the problems of congestion and traffic flow. There have been various attempts at decongesting the city centre; some of the narrow streets and squares in the main tourist areas have been pedestrianised (e.g. around the Pantheon and the Trevi Fountain, so, too, some of the shopping streets around the Via del Corso, Rome's high street).

In the 1970s and 1980s, various attempts were made to restrain traffic from entering the city centre. One trial plan reduced traffic flows by 50 per cent by allowing cars bearing odd and even number plates into the *centro storico* on alternate days; another allowed only cars with specific permits to enter the centre. Both systems failed as they were not properly enforced.

Various plans to build large, underground car parks have been put forward, but few have been realised; as with other schemes which involve excavations in the centre of Rome, archaeological remains are likely to be disturbed. In the mid 1990s the city started its first trial 'pay and display' parking areas (blue zones). The success of these remains to be seen; as with the correct use of bus lanes, orderly parking is a part of the long-term education of the average Roman motorist, discouraging them from their traditional anarchic habits.

PUBLIC TRANSPORT

In order to discourage car drivers from the roads, public transport needs to be improved. In 1950, when Rome had only 32 000 cars, there was a comprehensive network of trams covering 140 km. The hosting of the Olympic Games in 1960 led to the dismembering of most of the network, in favour of a new one-way system for motor traffic. The fuel crisis of 1975 led to some tram lines being reinstated. In 1990, a new 'supertram' link was built between central Rome and the Olympic Stadium, where the World Cup was being held and another supertram is being built for the Holy Year 'Jubilee' in the year 2000. The story of the trams reflects the piecemeal nature of planning in Rome – new projects are conceived when big international events are to be held rather than for the long-term day-to-day functioning of the city.

Rome has one of the least developed underground railway systems for a major European city (see Figure 11.4). The first *metropolitana* (underground) line was projected by Mussolini's Fascist regime during the 1930s; however, the war intervened and it was finally opened in 1955. The second line took 26 years to build, opening in 1980. One of the main hold ups was the frequent discovery of archaeological remains which needed proper excavation before work could continue (as

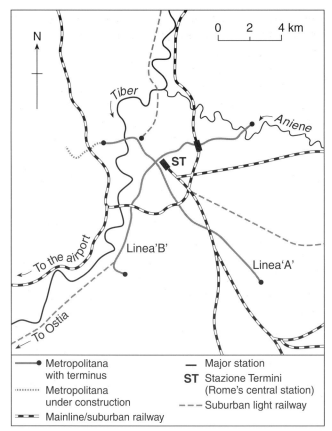

Figure 11.4 *Rome's 'metro' network*

graphically illustrated in Fellini's film *Roma*). With 33 km of track and 43 stations, the metro is one of the cheapest in Europe and is well patronised (190 million passengers per year), but only a small percentage of Romans live within easy reach of a station. At present, although two more lines are planned, slow-moving, polluting buses remain the main form of public transport.

Suburban sections of the main line railways have become a more important part of Rome's public transport network in recent years. Parts of the FS (national railway company) track have been designated as *Ferrovie Metropolitane* (Metropolitan Railways) and are integrated into the city's public transport and ticketing systems. These lines provide important commuter links between the towns and villages of the Roman *Campagna* and the city centre; the volume of traffic reflects the degree to which Rome is undergoing counterurbanisation.

MONUMENTS AND POLLUTION

Rome has the biggest concentration of historic monuments of any European capital. The places of historic interest fall into two main categories: the ancient Roman remains, including the Forum, the Colosseum and the Pantheon, and those belonging

to the great rebuilding of Rome in the Baroque period, including St Peter's Basilica, the Spanish Steps and Piazza Navona. Central Rome has over 200 churches and 200 palaces, all needing to be maintained and periodically restored. The deterioration of these monuments has been more rapid in the last few decades than in previous centuries, purely because of the fumes and vibrations from motor traffic.

There are 10 pollution monitoring units within the city which measure daily levels of carbon monoxide, nitrogen dioxide, sulphur dioxide, ozone and particulate material. As Rome has few industrial plants, the vast majority of the pollution comes from motor traffic (with a small amount from oil central heating in the winter months). The ideal conditions

Figure 11.5 *The replica statue of Marcus Aurelius on the Capitoline Hill*

under which air pollution levels become a health risk occur during the warmer months, following several days of windless, anticyclone weather.

Money is constantly being spent on restoration of monuments and comes from a variety of sources including the State, the *comune* (municipal authority), the EU and the income from tourism. Certain outdoor works of art, such as the bronze statue of Marcus Aurelius on the Capitoline Hill, have suffered so much corrosion that they have been removed and replaced by replicas. The time taken for monuments to be restored can be frustrating for tourists; it is not unusual for a building, an art gallery or an archaeological site to be closed to the public for more than 20 years.

One possible remedy for at least some of the air pollution has been the introduction of non-polluting battery operated electric buses in the city centre; however, the long-term solution must be the reduction of all motor traffic.

Another potential threat to Rome's monuments is Italy's tectonic instability. Several earthquakes were responsible for demolishing part of the Colosseum in late Roman times; much more recently parts of the Forum became unsafe suring the Norcia earthquake of 1979 and damage was done to frescoes in Rome's churches during the Foligno earthquake of October 1997.

EMPLOYMENT

Rome is unique among large Italian cities in having such a large proportion of its workforce in the tertiary sector, and such a small percentage in secondary. (Only 16 per cent of Rome's workforce is engaged in manufacturing, as opposed to over 45 per cent in both Milan and Turin.) The city was deliberately prevented from becoming heavily industrialised, first by the Popes who ruled Rome until 1870, and then by successive Italian governments. Effectively, Rome has 'leap frogged' from a pre-industrial to a post-industrial economy. What industry Rome has is generally small scale and traditional, including furniture making, luxury goods, clothing, printing, food processing, building materials and construction. In recent decades, the city has attracted high-tech industries to its suburban fringe. In the 1930s, the Fascist regime developed a ring of industrial towns in the Lazio region, where heavier industries are still located. Rome's most important industrial satellite town is Pomezia, 43 km to the south-east, which has enjoyed the tax benefits of being located just within the boundary of the *Cassa per il Mezzogiorno,* Italy's regional development fund for the South.

Around 250 000 people are involved in administration in Rome, as state officials employed at all levels of government. Added to this are the bureaucrats who work in the private sector, in banking and commerce and for the Roman Catholic Church and the United Nations. Other forms of tertiary employment include transport and the tourist industry.

Unemployment stands at around 12 per cent, although it is difficult to calculate because of the tradition in Mediterranean economies of many people being semi-employed, unofficially employed or having several part-time jobs. Certain trends are changing the pattern of employment:

- The proposed scaling down of government bureaucracy will lead to higher unemployment.
- Economic restructuring is having a bad effect upon small businesses. These have been traditionally strong in Rome and are capable of absorbing unemployed workers.

- Large-scale immigration, much of it illegal, from LEDCs has led to thousands of poorly paid jobs no longer being in Italian hands which, in turn, has led to racial tensions within the city. (Current estimates are that among foreigners working in Rome there are 25 000 from the Philippines, 7000 Egyptians, 5500 from Sri Lanka and 4500 Ethiopians.)
- The trend towards decentralisation is taking certain functions and, therefore, jobs out of Rome (e.g. the wholesale markets are moving to Guidonia, 24 km to the north-east of the city; the Bank of Italy is also due to move out to a more rural area). Such moves are merely stimulating the counterurbanisation process.

HOUSING

Heavy immigration to Rome from the surrounding rural areas and from the South of Italy in the 1930s led to the development of the first large *borgate* or poor suburbs. The high-rise blocks in such districts as Magliana, Turfello and Pietralata were constructed in the Fascist period to accommodate migrant workers. From the 1950s to the mid 1970s when even heavier migration took place, some 85 *borgate* sprang up around Rome. Many of the classic social realism films of Pasolini are set in these *borgate.* Owners of plots of agricultural land made fortunes from speculative developments. Although the city has a regulatory plan, the time taken to get through the bureaucracy led people to build without planning permission.

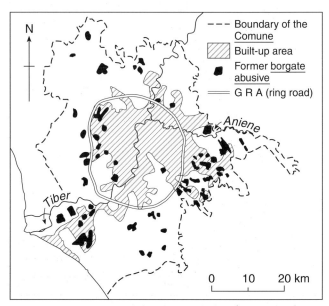

Figure 11.6 *Rome's ex* borgate abusive

By 1981, when Rome's population peaked, there were an estimated 300 000 people living in so-called *case abusive* (illegally built houses). Figure 11.6 shows the extent of such developments around the city.

Various Italian town planners have likened the situation to the shanty towns of Latin America. Housing was built without provision for basic services such as schools, street lighting, shops, public parks and properly surfaced roads. The desolate landscapes of half-finished, high-rise blocks, rubble and wasteland are a world apart from the elegant streets of central Rome. Some of the illegally built areas were demolished, but most were given an amnesty and, as in the case of Latin American shanties, the city authorities have upgraded the areas, laying on the basic amenities. However, the *borgate* have become areas with severe social problems: high rates of unemployment, street crime, vandalism, drug abuse and enviromental degradation, even though, for the first generation of migrants, they would have offered cheap but comfortable housing and better job prospects than in their home areas.

Throughout Rome there is a shortage of housing, even though thousands of flats remain empty. Fair rent laws favouring the tenant have discouraged

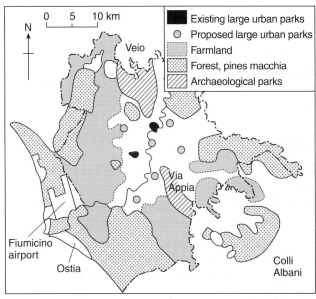

Figure 11.8 *Rome's Green Belt*

landlords from letting their properties. In the *centro storico*, gentrification has been taking place in the last few decades, transforming some of the traditionally working-class districts such as Trastevere into areas where the rich are forcing out the poor.

Since Rome has been experiencing moderate counterurbanisation, some 100 000 people have left the city for the surrounding towns, villages and countryside to get away from the pollution and congestion. This search for a better lifestyle has led to the rapid expansion of lakeside towns such as Bracciano, towns in the hills such as Velletri and seaside towns such as Nettuno.

AN OVERALL PLAN?

Despite having had many official strategic plans, Rome suffers from a lack of consistent planning. Too

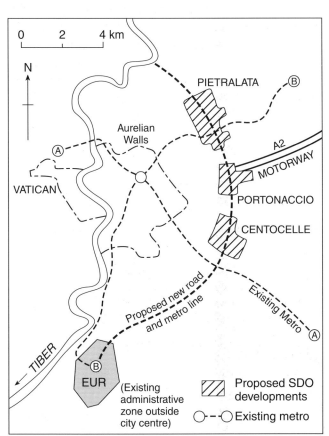

Figure 11.7 *Proposed location of the SDO*

Figure 11.9 *Speculative 1960s housing*

the urban problems of Rome

many changes are made on a piecemeal basis as a reaction to a crisis or to a special event. The city government is often an unstable coalition and to make matters worse there are four layers of administration in Rome: national, regional, provincial and municipal – complicating the decision-making process and adding to the bureaucracy.

One of the most significant plans of recent decades was that of the 'SDO' (*Sistema Direzionale Orientale*), first put forward in 1962, but finally abandoned in 1995. The project would have moved all of the Ministries from the centre of Rome to a new, purpose-built site in the eastern suburbs (see Figure 11.7). As well as government and other services, the SDO would have provided housing for 225 000 people and new, fast road and metro links. The plan was controversial, swallowed up large sums of money and never materialised.

Many a grand scheme has been put forward for the Holy Year 'Jubilee' of 2000, just as for the failed Olympic Games bid for 2004. A planned new metro line to link the Vatican with the Colosseum (Rome's two most important tourist venues), in time for the Holy Year fell through because of lack of advanced planning. Similarly, the plan for a motor traffic tunnel under part of Central Rome has been abandoned. Although money is available, plans for the millennium have been scaled right down and there are fears that Rome will not be able to accommodate all the extra pilgrims and tourists.

Figure 11.10 *A new electric minibus in the 'centro storico'*

In 1992, Rome elected its first ever Green Party mayor, Francesco Rutelli. Many far reaching ideas have been put forward, including a proper Green Belt for the city (see Figure 11.8). This would be one of the largest in Europe, covering 82 000 ha and combining agricultural land, the gardens attached to former aristocratic mansions, natural woodlands and areas of archaeological importance within the countryside.

The present town administration has had certain success at the neighbourhood level in improving the efficiency of local services (health, housing, rubbish disposal, etc.) and in cutting down on the complex bureaucracy. Improvements may be made slowly and on a small scale, but the almost intractable problem of the 'Eternal City' seem to prevent any long-term grand plan from being a success.

SUMMARY

- City at least 2750 years old
- Since 1950 rapid expansion into the *Campagna* (countryside)
- 2.79 million people, 2 million motor vehicles
- Congested mediaeval street pattern in the *centro storico*
- Limited pedestrianisation
- Ill-developed metro (33 km); recent intergration with suburban trains
- Very high pollution levels destroying monuments
- 200 churches and 200 palaces to be maintained
- Low employment in industry (16 per cent)
- 250 000 people in administration
- High unemployment (12 per cent); greater underemployment
- Recent large-scale immigration from LEDCs
- 85 illegally built *borgate* with 300 000 inhabitants in 1980s
- Difficulties in overall planning/decision making
- SDO project to decongest the centre abandoned
- Planned Green Belt of 82 000 ha

EXAMINATION
QUESTIONS

This case study can be of direct application to syllabus sections on managing cities, urban development, urban problems and associated issues. Although Rome is an MEDC city many of its problems are similar to those in LEDC cities. Indeed, this case study could be used to good effect as a contrast to somewhere in Northern Europe or to somewhere in an LEDC.

SPECIFIC

Examples of questions for which this case study can be used directly:

1 With reference to one or more cities you have studied, outline the main planning problems which may be encountered as a result of recent urban growth.

2 To what extent does the location and growth pattern of a city influence the lives of its inhabitants?

GENERAL

More general use of this case study, in combination with others could include answering questions such as:

3 To what extent do the cities of Less Economically Developed Countries face a different range of problems from cities in More Economically Developed Countries?

4 'Housing and Employment are the two greatest problems encountered in cities in LEDCs.' To what extent is this also true in cities in MEDCs?

— CASE STUDY — 12

CAIRO: AFRICA'S GREATEST METROPOLIS

> **Barely 50 metres away [from a modern office], begins a labyrinth of narrow lanes where millions of Egyptians live in seedy shacks and dark warrens above and below ground, often without water, sewers or electricity ...**
>
> *Amos Elon, One Foot on the Moon*

Cairo, with an estimated population of between 11 and 14 million inhabitants, is not only by far the largest city in Africa but is also one of the continent's oldest continuously occupied settlements. The city owes its importance both to its location on the River Nile at the strategic point before it divides to flow into its fertile delta, and to the succession of civilisations which have ruled over Egypt at various stages in history.

As with other great cities in LEDCs, Cairo has immense problems associated with its growth, housing and employment, its transport system, basic services and waste disposal. Despite acute poverty in some quarters, it is one of the most

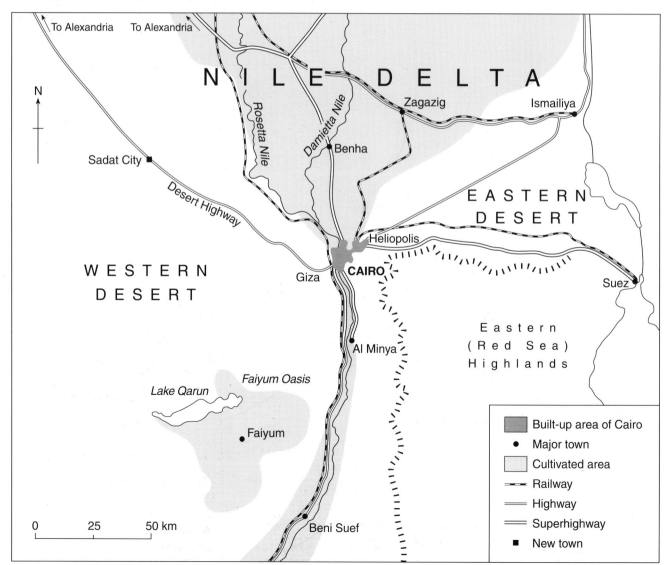

Figure 12.1 *Location of Cairo*

fascinating of capitals in Africa and, with a history which goes back almost 5000 years, has numerous buildings and monuments of world importance.

LOCATION OF CAIRO

Cairo is located 200 km from the North African coast where the waters of the two branches of the River Nile drain into the Mediterranean Sea. Some 20 km to the north-west of the city centre the two distributaries (the Rosetta Nile and the Damietta Nile) branch out and provide irrigation water for the highly productive delta farmlands which help to feed the burgeoning population of Egypt's 'megacity'. Figure 12.1 shows the regional position of Cairo.

In the centre of Cairo there are a number of islands where the channel of the Nile is braided; these, in fact, made Cairo's location favourable as an easy crossing point for ferries. However, until the various barrages were constructed across the river further upstream during the late 19th and early 20th centuries, the Nile continued to flood during the

summer and thereby constantly changed its shape and course, in what is now central Cairo. This explains why the more historic parts of the city were built away from the river's edge where its flow was unpredictable. Within a few kilometres of the right bank of the Nile is the elevated land of the Jebel Muqattam and Jebel Tura, both extensions of the Red Sea Highlands; they have the effect of making the valley of the Nile quite narrow at this point, which historically gave Cairo easy control of the main north-south routeway.

HISTORY, DEVELOPMENT AND FUNCTION ZONES OF CAIRO

Cairo has seen a succession of cities at this point along the course of the Nile, most of which have been absorbed into the fabric of the present city. Each successive settlement has enlarged the built-up area of the city, added new functions and changed the character of Cairo. What was a desirable residential or commercial area in one century may decline into

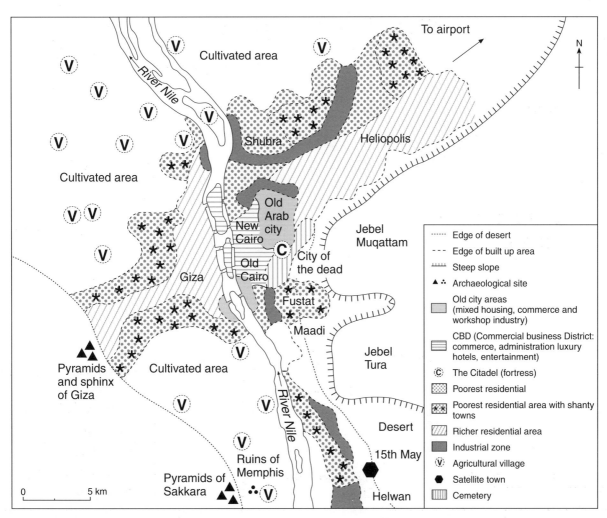

Figure 12.2 *The structure of Cairo*

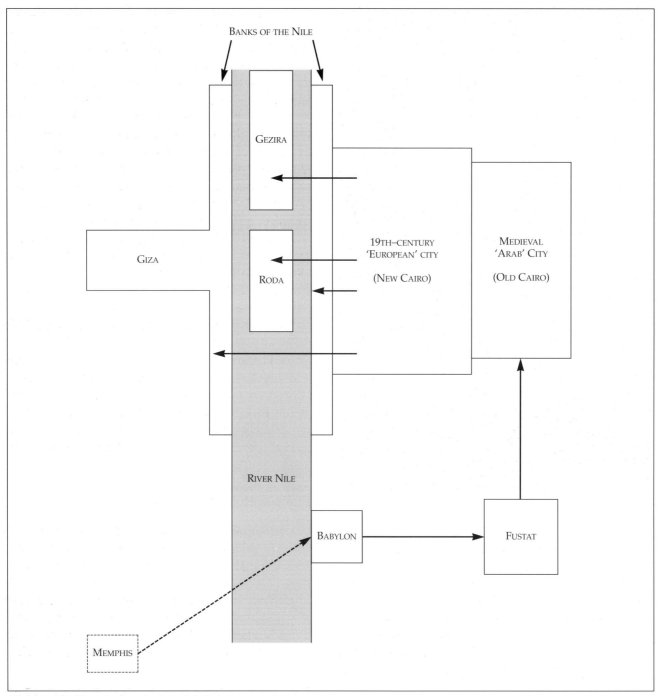

File 12.3 *The historical evolution of Cairo's core area*

a poor district at a later date. Figures 12.2 and 12.3 show the present structure of the city and how it can be explained in terms of its gradual evolution.

The first settlement of major importance in the Cairo region was Memphis, the capital of the united kingdoms of Upper and Lower Egypt. On the west bank of the Nile, some 15 km from central Cairo, Memphis was at the height of its power around 2500 BC; it is now just a series of ruined temples and tombs opposite the industrial suburb of Helwan, but it is an important part of the international tourist

circuit along with neighbouring Sakkara and the Pyramids at Giza.

On the right bank of the Nile, 3 km from central Cairo is 'Babylon-in-Egypt', also known as 'Old Cairo'. This was an important walled city in Roman times but today has declined into being one of the poorer inner suburbs where the minority Coptic Christian community is concentrated. Housing in this area is overcrowded and often lacking basic amenities.

In the 7th century, the Moslems built a new city to the east of Babylon, known as Fustat. Today, this has flood-waters of the Nile, the CBD of Cairo shifted westwards when the so-called 'European City' was laid out during the period of colonial rule and modernisation. Wide, tree-lined boulevards were laid out in a geometric pattern in this area where banks, large shops, commercial and administrative offices, cafés and restaurants, as well as luxury apartment blocks for middle-class Cairenes were all located. This area now lacks its former vitality and is rather run down and degraded, as a result of the more prestigious businesses relocating in modern office blocks and the rich moving out to residential suburbs such as Heliopolis and Maadi.

Since the mid 20th century, Cairo has spread and sprawled in many directions. The CBD functions have moved even closer to the Nile, finally controlled by the building of the Aswan High Dam. Banks and international corporations, luxury hotels and apartment blocks now line the banks of the Nile on both sides of the river and on the Gezira and Roda Islands. Further hotels, cinemas, resturants and night clubs line the main boulevard through Giza, on the road to the Pyramids; these are aimed at the lucrative Middle Eastern market and have established Cairo as the 'pleasure capital' of the region since the demise of Beirut during the Lebanese conflict.

POPULATION AND HOUSING

Cairo is growing at a rate of 300 000 to 350 000 people per year, both from natural increase (which for Egypt is 2.1 per cent per annum), and from heavy rural–urban migration, most of which is unofficial. Some estimates suggest that 39 per cent of Egypt's population lives within the GCR (Greater Cairo Region), which would make Cairo one of the most extreme examples of urban primacy in Africa.

Figure 12.4 *The 19th-century European city*

become degraded into one of the poorest districts of the city, where large numbers of new migrants live in shanty-town areas which, like a vision of 'hell on earth', surround the smoking furnaces of the city's main brick and pottery kilns.

To the north, the Arab conquerors built two more new cities, *El Qata'iyeh* in the area around the Ibn Tulun Mosque and *El Qahira*, meaning 'the Victorious', from which the present city's name derives. These two areas are known generally as the 'Arab City' and include most of Cairo's historic core, with mosques, bazaars, merchants' houses, the Islamic university and the fortified citadel perched high above on the edge of Jebel Muqattam. This was, until the late 19th century, the main commercial and administrative centre of Cairo, the home of the prosperous middle classes, as well as the poorer artisans and shopkeepers. Today, it is an area of high population density from which the rich have moved out and the poor have moved in, with traditional merchants' courtyard houses subdivided into often squalid living quarters.

In the 19th century, with the gradual taming of the

Figure 12.5 *The medieval 'Arab' city*

The Egyptian capital now stretches over 25 km from Giza in the west to Heliopolis in the east, and for almost 40 km from the north to south along the valley of the Nile. Most of this expansion has been valuable arable land around villages which became absorbed into the urban fabric; over 750 ha of farmland are lost each year by urbanisation.

Where expansion cannot take place outwards, it has to go upwards, with ever higher blocks of flats erected to cope with population pressure. Tenement blocks of 20 storeys are now common in many parts of Cairo, whereas in the 1980s 10 storeys was usually the maximum height. This gives some of the poorer, overcrowded parts of the city population densities of 100 000 per km^2, and even the average for the GCR is 40 000 per km^2. It is common for private speculators building high-rise blocks to add extra storeys as and when they can afford the necessary materials. This leaves so much of the skyline of Cairo with a 'half-finished' appearance. Squatters settle in simple shelters on rooftops throughout the poorer quarters, and it is believed that as many as 1 million Cairenes live on the roofs of the city, sometimes together with their goats and chickens. For people living in this way, rainfall poses few problems, but the winter nights may be bitterly cold.

Housing is frequently sub-standard, contravening what few easily enforceable building regulations there are in Cairo. The collapse of badly constructed multi-storey blocks of flats and other buildings led to the unnecessary loss of life during the 1992 Cairo earthquake. Figure 12.6 is a newspaper report of the event.

The shortage of housing is made worse by tenacy laws which were introduced to protect the poor. A flat may be let to one specific family for two or three generations on a 50-year fixed rent. At the same time, new tenants may be charged extortionate rents and huge deposits for a property. Such a situation leads to some properties remaining unlet, while some become the homes of squatters, and others become illegal sub-lets for extremely high rents.

The desperation for accommodation in Cairo has led to the colonisation of the city's cemeteries by families who have nowhere else to live. Adjacent to the mediaeval quarters, on the edge of the eastern desert, are two large cemetaries known as the 'City of the Dead'. Inside are numerous old house tombs belonging to the richer Cairene families; these provide shelter and homes for up to 1 million people. Shanty towns in Cairo often miss out on

Figure 12.7 *A street vendor in the Khan-el-Kalili Bazaar*

certain basic public amenities. The 'City of the Dead', not surprisingly, lacked the services needed by the living. However, as in other squatter areas, the local authorities have provided various amenities such as water and electricity supplies for some of the tomb dwellers; the 'City of the Dead' now also boasts a police station, a post office, several schools and various bus routes to other parts of the city.

Despite so much degradation of building in the Arab mediaeval quarters, there are some moves afoot to re-evaluate and upgrade some districts, although it will probably be many decades before there is any European-style gentrification of the historic core. The Gamaliya district, between the city walls and the main Khan el Khalili bazaar (which is well patronised by both Cairenes and tourists), contains a large number of fine, but poorly preserved, mediaeval Islamic monuments such as mosques, monasteries, palaces and colleges. Families and small artisan businesses were involved in discussions to decide how to revitalise the area, and the 'Sustainable Development Association of Gamaliya' was set up. This is a community scheme which is involved in the development of craft industries, (including the training of women), the restoring of old buildings, the cleaning up of the area by moving out certain polluting functions and the stimulation of tourist interest in the area.

PUBLIC SERVICES

It is not only the shanty towns which lack good public services but most of the city has problems resulting from poor amenities. Rapid population growth, hurried building projects using cheap materials, the shortage of funding and the lack of planning all put stress upon the infrastructure of

Mubarak flies back to political fallout

PRESIDENT Mubarak cut short a visit to China and flew back to Cairo last night as the earthquake death toll rose above the 400 level. Thousands camped out on the road to the airport preparing to flee the country amid rumours of aftershocks. Yitzhak Rabin, the Israeli prime minister, telephoned Mr Mubarak last night to express his country's sorrow at the disaster and offered "any help needed".

The city was in a state of shock as its 12 million inhabitants struggled to cope with the implications of the country's worst earthquake. Because of mass hysteria and shoddy building, many more people were killed than might have been expected in a medium-sized tremor. The first to make political capital were the Islamic extremists who have been mounting a growing challenge to President Mubarak. They began circulating the damning message in the most overcrowded and badly hit areas that the damage was the wrath of Allah inflicted on a corrupt administration.

One man predicted that, within weeks, there would be street protests against the government, which is being blamed for the lax regulations that allowed so many landlords to get away with poor construction by contravening building regulations.

In the filthy wards of Cairo's main Qasr al-Aini hospital, 330 men, women and children were recovering after the earthquake. "The sad truth is that the vast majority of the people brought here were injured in the panic stampedes which followed the earthquake", said Dr Omar Rashad a lecturer at the country's largest university teaching hospital.

One patient, Abdel Halim Abu Rabia, 75, a devout Muslim, had been preparing for afternoon prayers in a suburban mosque when the earthquake struck. He was trampled by fellow worshippers who abandoned him with a broken leg.

A similar fate awaited Fathi Ibrahim, a furniture polisher in central Cairo, who rushed out of his workshop and remembers little else. Later he discovered that a deep head wound requiring stitches was caused by a panic-stricken mob that knocked him over and left him for dead.

Many victims apparently owe their misfortune as much to building contractors and slum landlords as to the quake. Most of Cairo, including the Sphinx at Giza, emerged unscathed, while cheap housing and at least one gerry-built 14-storey block of flats collapsed because landlords were too poor or too greedy to bother about foundations.

Salma Eid, 10, emerged with only cuts and bruises when her lesson in religious studies was interrupted by the quake and she was trampled under the feet of fleeing classmates, though the tremor did not cause even a crack in the school walls. Thirty-four children were killed in a similar stampede at the Asmeh school in the slum of Shubra.

Amid Hogarthian scenes of scavenging dogs and stinking, half-burning rubbish tips, panic-stricken children yesterday told how their schoolmates had been killed and 67 of them has been injured in a mass stampede. "The teachers panicked and then ran away, telling everyone else to do the same," said Salem, 12, as he stood outside the school which, like all those run by the state, has been closed for 72 hours. "The children were trampled to death. It was a terrible sight."

Other children, gathered outside the locked metal gates of the three-storey building, pointed out the obvious, that it was still standing, with broken windows about the only structural damage apparent. "The building shook. Everybody ran and that is why they were killed," said Muhammad Ashraf, a man in his thirties.

In an attempt to defuse popular discontent. Atef Sidki the prime minister, announced a grant of 500 Egyptian pounds (£88) for each death and a further 200 pounds for each injury. As parents queued with a touch of fatalism to collect cash payments, Egyptian red tape was again in evidence. Officials in the garden of the Nile hospital told Sayyid Radwan, 43, a factory worker who had lost his daughter, Fatma, that he should have stayed the day before to claim his cash. They then sent him back inside the building for two more signatures on his compensation form.

Figure 12.6 *Article from the* **The Times** *14 October 1992*

Cairo. The earthquake of 1992 merely highlighted the great problems which already existed. Electricity and water supplies can be erratic: power cuts are frequent occurrences in various parts of the city; where water is piped, pressure is deliberately kept low to avoid burst mains in the decaying pipe network. Where there are no water mains, houses rely upon horse-drawn delivery tankers, whose visits are irregular. Sewage and rubbish disposal are two other services where the urban authorities fail to meet the need. Even more serious are the decaying, overcrowded schools and hospitals in the poorer districts such as Shubra and Imbaba.

In such areas, poverty and discontent at the falling living standards and lack of welfare have led to urban rioting. Some quarters have, therefore, almost become 'no go' areas for the authorities. This is where the radical Islamic groups have stepped in, seizing upon the opportunity to expose the failures of the present system. Religious groups have voluntarily taken over the running of some of the ramshackle schools and clinics, so it is not surprising that militant Islam is on the rise in Cairo. In 1992, it was the Muslim Brotherhood, rather than the government, which stepped in to provide tents and food for those made homeless by the earthquake.

Where the 'formal' sector such as the city authorities cannot provide, an 'informal' sector is likely to evolve to take its place. This has happened in the case of rubbish disposal in Cairo. Cairenes generate 6000 tonnes of solid waste each day. Half of this is collected and disposed of by the *zabbaleen*, poor landless migrants from Upper Egypt who established themselves in the city more than 50 years ago. They live in seven settlements dotted around Cairo, the largest of which is under the Muqattam Hill near the 'City of the Dead'. The

zabbaleen are Coptic Christians and this enables them, unlike Muslims, to keep pigs which feed off and dispose of the rotting organic matter.

In poor cities such as Cairo, the waste materials are seen as valuable and are sorted into cloth, paper, glass and plastic and carefully processed ready to be sent for recycling. The *zabbaleen* have developed simple technologies for reclaiming and recycling materials; the men and children collect the rubbish and the women are involved in the sorting. Now they are a well-organised sector of the economy with 7000 *zabbaleen* belonging to the Association of Rubbish Collectors for Community Development. This provides training, healthcare and loans to its members, which the state cannot.

TRANSPORT PROBLEMS

Cairo has the same transport problems as many other capital cities in LEDCs, but the sheer physical and population size of the metropolitan area makes these problems more acute. In the city centre, traffic congestion is the major problem, with lorries, buses, taxis, private cars and horse-drawn vehicles all vying for space. Pollution levels are high because of the desert climate and the widespread use of diesel vehicles. Broad boulevards in the European city and narrow streets in the Arab city alike become blocked during rush hours.

Rameses Square, where Cairo's main station is located, and other parts of the city centre are dominated by huge, ugly flyovers; this was the 1970s solution to the congestion problem. One factor that made matters worse was the amount of through traffic between Upper Egypt and Alexandria, which was forced to go through the centre of Cairo before the building of the ring road, started in 1985. The ring road itself has become another major problem for Cairo.

Figure 12.8 shows the proposed development of the route of the ring road. It would have been a 72 km long, eight-lane motorway which would have passed within a few hundred metres of the Pyramids and Sphynx at Giza. Following protests from UNESCO, President Mubarak put a stop to construction of the Giza section in 1995. Not only would the road have caused degradation by pollution and vibration to one of the world's most important heritage sites but would have prevented further excavations under the tarmac-covered area.

In solving some of the traffic congestion in its centre, Cairo became the first African city to have an underground metro system. The present

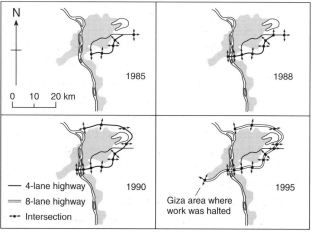

Figure 12.8 *Growth stages of Cairo's ring road*

underground stretch is just 3 km long under CBD and links two former suburban railway lines. Further expansion of the metro is planned, together with additional tram routes.

NEW TOWNS AND NEW HIERARCHIES

In 1969, President Nasser launched a plan to create four new settlements in the Cairo region in order to relieve some of the pressure from the capital's urban growth. Over time, this plan became more complex and a total of 14 new towns at different scales with different functions was projected. This would, in fact, eventually produce a totally new hierarchy of settlement within Lower Egypt.

Only three of the originally envisaged satellite towns were established – 6th October, Al Obout and 15th May. These were all within 40 km of Cairo and had population targets of 250 000 to 500 000. Essentially, these towns still rely upon Cairo for much of their employment and some of their major services.

At a greater distance from Cairo are the four larger new towns which were planned to have an eventual population of between 500 000 and 1 million. Two of these, 10th Ramadan and Al Badr, were located within the Greater Cairo Region, Sadat City was located on the Desert Highway between Cairo and Alexandria, whereas New Aneriya was built within the sphere of influence of Alexandria. These towns are, in theory, to be more self-contained in terms of employment than the satellite towns.

The various new towns are positioned along 'development corridors', roads which link Cario to other major centres of population (e.g. 10th Ramadan is located on the desert road to Ismailiya). Generally, new towns are designed to be centres of manufacturing industry, although 6th October's location means that it will also be associated with new developments in Egypt's tourist industry. (Figure 12.9 locates the main towns in Egypt's new settlement heirarchy.)

10th Ramadan has proved to be a success story, partly because of its proximity to Cairo. At a distance of 55 km from the capital, it has attracted much more new industry than Sadat City which is 96 km away. Set up in 1977, 10th Ramadan had attracted 531 industrial plants by 1993, with another 263 factories under construction; this has generated 36 000 jobs, with an additional 16 000 to follow. The nature of the employment, together with the wages (30 per cent above those for skilled workers in Cairo), have encouraged commuting from the

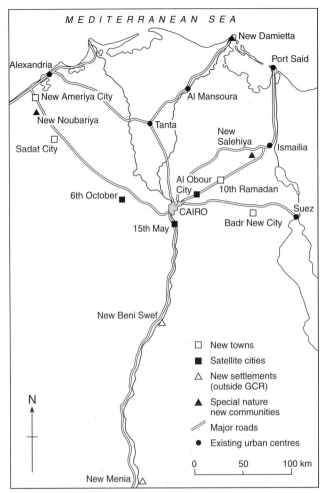

Figure 12.9 *New urban hierarchy of Lower Egypt*

capital, which accounts for 40 per cent of 10th Ramadan's workforce. Similarly, there is heavy commuting in the opposite direction. Such statistics show that the new towns are rather defeating the *raison d'être* of their foundation.

Figure 12.10 shows the structure of the 10th Ramadan development. The overall plan and cellular way in which it is evolving shows a more imaginative approach than in the new towns of many other countries.

In some of the new towns the provision of public services has been poor; water and electrictiy supplies and public transport often fail to meet the demands of the inhabitants. The biggest problem in 10th Ramadan is water supply. Daily, 70 000 m³ of water have to be brought in from the Ismailiya Canal, but this meets only 25 per cent of the town's needs. The water supply for the entire city is closed off from 11 p.m. until 5 a.m. each day.

Although housing in 10th Ramadan is, in general, of a higher standard than in the poorer districts of Cairo from where most of the migrants to new

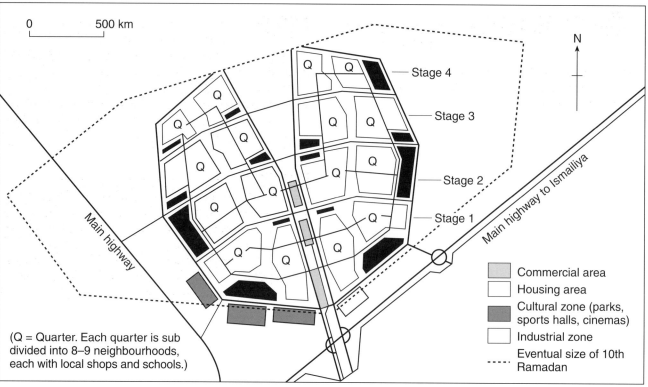

Figure 12.10 *Layout of 10th Ramdan new town*

towns originate, a considerable amount of the housing stock remains unoccupied. Speculative purchasing of whole blocks by wealthy Cairenes is one of the main reasons for this.

There may be teething troubles with these new towns which will last for decades, but they are having considerable success in taking the pressures away from Cairo itself.

SUMMARY

- Population between 11 and 14 million
- Located near the branching of the Nile
- A succession of commercial cores
- Present CBD close to Nile which no longer floods
- Problems of substandard housing, shown in 1992 earthquake
- Basic services and amenities lacking
- *Zabbaleen* act as unoffical rubbish collectors
- The first underground metro in Africa
- 72 km ring road halted around the Pyramids
- 14 new towns planned
- 10th Ramadan most successful

●— EXAMINATION — QUESTIONS

Cairo is an excellent example of an LEDC city full of problems. This case study may have wider economic geography applications.

SPECIFIC

Direct questions could include:

1 With reference to specific case studies, what are the main problems facing LEDC cities and how may they be solved?

2 What is the role played by new towns in urban planning? Assess their success in one or more areas you have studied.

GENERAL

More general application of this case study might be:

3 With reference to specific countries, examine the problems they encounter which may hold back their economic development.

4 Rural–urban migration is one of the greatest causes of poverty in LEDCs. Examine this with relation to specific cities you have studied.

— CASE STUDY — ⓭ THE INDUSTRIAL AND ECONOMIC DEVELOPMENT OF SINGAPORE

1995 was the year of graduation which never took place. At first the media announced that the OECD had reclassified Singapore as having graduated to their ranks .... But we then discovered it had been a mistake. We learnt later that the OECD had actually reclassified Singapore as a 'more advanced developing country', a kind of halfway house between developing and developed status.

Ho Kwon Ping, Wah Chang International Group

Although Mr Ho's statement suggests that Singapore might have an identity crisis, it has one of the most successful economies in the Far East. Despite its modest origins, Singapore has emerged as an economic powerhouse within South East Asia and, as one of the four original 'Tiger Economies' of the region, is seen as a model for successful development. Today, its per capita GNP ($ US 26 730) is the third largest in Asia, after Japan and oil-rich Brunei. As an island republic of just 2.9 million people, its success has been due to a good geographical location rather than to its natural resources, and to the way in which the Singapore government has adopted a rigid planning strategy towards its economic development.

GEOGRAPHICAL BACKGROUND

Singapore has an area of just 647.5 km² and is made up of the main Singapore Island together with a few dozen smaller offshore islands, although the area is gradually being extended as reclamation projects

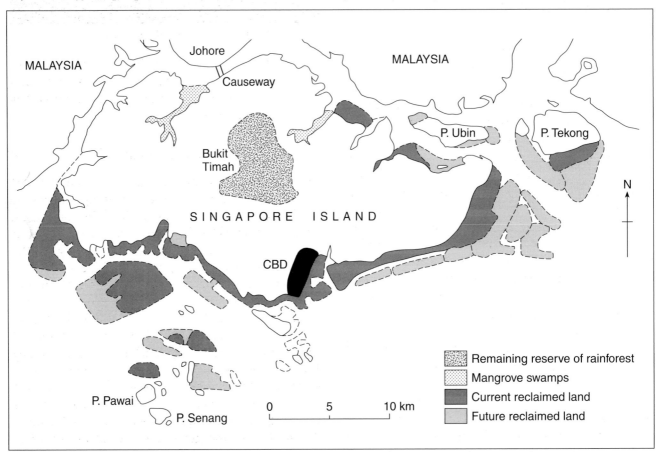

Figure 13.1 *Singapore Island*

take place. The country is located approximately 1° N of the equator and, consequently, has a hot, humid climate throughout the year, with average daytime temperatures around 31°C and a total annual rainfall of 2400 mm. Once covered in dense tropical rainforest, few areas survive in their natural state, the most notable being the Bukit Timah Nature Reserve in the centre of the island. Along the coasts there are several muddy creeks which harbour primary mangrove swamps (see Figure 13.1).

Singapore's geographical position is the key to its economic success. Located at the southern tip of the Malay Peninsula, it owes its growth and development to the important trade routes which grew up between Europe, the Far East and beyond in the 18th and 19th centuries. These shipping routes are funnelled through the narrow Straits of Malacca, between the Malaysian mainland and the Indonesian island of Sumatra. Earlier, as a producer and processor of rubber and other raw materials, later as an entrepôt and now as a modern industrial and commercial centre, Singapore has enjoyed economic success from being in such a nodal position.

HISTORICAL BACKGROUND

In the early 18th century, Singapura ('Lion City'), was a part of the Malay sultanate of Malacca. At the time, Britain ruled over India and its trade with China was growing rapidly. A port of call was needed to refit and protect the merchant fleet, and in 1819 the settlement of Singapore was founded by Sir Stamford Raffles. The port soon prospered and by 1832 Singapore was the capital of the group of British colonies in the area known as the Straits Settlements. With the opening of the Suez Canal in 1869, trade boomed and by the end of the 19th century Singapore had become the world centre of the newly important rubber trade. Trade expanded eight-fold between 1873 and 1913, leading to the influx of migrant workers from Malaya, India and, in particular, from China. This migration underlies the current ethnic structure of Singapore, a 77 per cent Chinese city within an otherwise Malay region.

After Japanese occupation during the Second World War, Singapore moved towards independence from Britain; self-governing from 1959, it briefly became part of the Federation of Malaysia in 1963. The ill-fated union was short-lived and the prime minister, Lee Kuan Yew, pulled Singapore out to go it alone in 1965. This small, isolated country was

Figure 13.2 *The high-rise CBD of Singapore*

then faced with a 'struggle for survival' and embarked upon a massive industrialisation programme, which paid off and laid the foundations for its present economic success.

THE INDUSTRIALISATION PROCESS

Singapore's thrust towards industrialisation could not have been achieved without a strong role played by the government through such institutions as the EDB (Economic Development Board) which was set up in 1961 to spearhead economic planning. At the same time, once Singapore was independent of Malaysia, it became necessary to create a sense of nationhood, so that the Chinese majority and the Malay and Indian (mainly Tamil) minorities would consider themselves, first and foremost Singaporeans. Ultimately, this has been achieved by huge increases in wealth, rising standards of education, the construction of good public housing and the other social benefits provided by the paternalistic style of government. As with the other Asian 'Tigers', the government used the threat of Communism and suspicion of the next-door neighbour (in this case Malaysia), to spur its people on to work hard for economic success and for the greater good of their new nation.

Singapore, like many other newly independent nations in the 1960s, adopted a policy of import substitution by developing heavy industries like iron and steel. This was not particularly appropriate for a small island state with few natural resources so Singapore encouraged Transnational Corporations (TNCs) to move in and set up processing plants which would specialise in goods for export. Two of the country's major advantages were the colonial legacy of an efficent infrastructure and a plentiful supply of cheap labour. Government action in 1968 make sure that the labour force would remain competitive by extending working hours, holding down wage levels and curbing trade union activites.

The two most important manufacturing sectors were initially petroleum products and textiles but, by the early 1970s, electronics became the boom industry, based mainly on the investments of US and Japanese parent companies (see Figure 13.4). Compared to the neighbouring countries which also had low labour costs, Singapore has a well-educated workforce ideal for the electronics industry. By 1973, manufactured goods overtook primary products as Singapore's main of exports. Manufacturing employment tripled between 1967 and 1973 and foreign firms were responsible for 75 per cent of output; at the same time many of Singapore's neighbours were lagging behind as they were reluctant to let in foreign companies. While industry was growing rapidly, so too was Singapore's role as an international financial centre.

After a short period of recession which coincided with the world oil crisis of 1974–5, Singapore embarked upon another phrase of economic expansion which it called its 'second industrial revolution'. By this time, the country was short of

Figure 13.3 *The container port, Singapore*

labour and was beginning to rely more and more on immigrant labour from neighbouring countries such as Malaysia, Indonesia and the Philippines.

At this time, the electronics industries in Korea, Taiwan and Hong Kong were a real competitive threat, so Singapore took the bold step to restructure wages upwards; between 1979 and 1984 there was a rise of 40 per cent in labour costs. This had the desired effect of increasing productivity and upgrading industries technologically. In the 1960s, the government had downgraded wages to be more competitive; it was now upgrading them in order to produce a superior labour force and, therefore, more sophisticated manufactured goods.

By the early 1990s the general standard of living of Singapore's workers had been transformed:

- the country experienced an average growth rate of 9 per cent per annum for over 30 years
- good, modern public housing provides homes for 80 per cent of the population (it was only 9 per cent in 1960)
- the state education system is successful
- the compulsory state savings scheme of 20 per cent of people's income provides for retirement pensions.

Some would argue that these achievements have not been made without restrictions on people's freedom; but this is looking at Singapore from a Western perspective rather than a Chinese one. The same political party, the PAP (Peoples' Action Party) has been in power since independence, English rather than Chinese has been adopted as the *de facto* national language, car ownership has been restricted by heavy import duties and there have been major public education campaigns against litter, chewing gum and other 'anti-social activites'. However draconian these measures, Singapore has been transformed into a clean, efficient, garden city – which makes it truly remarkable when compared with any other city so close to the equator.

Singapore is increasingly becoming a centre of tertiary activity, as a regional headquarters for banking (142 different banks operate there), trading, insurance and investment companies. However, unlike Britain in the 1980s, Singapore has not let the manufacturing sector decline as services have grown. Once again, government action is responsible for this by legislating that manufacturing should account for around 25 per cent of the GDP and 20 per cent of the workforce.

Whereas the service sector has been growing at an average of 8.3 per cent per annum over recent

	Percentage of total output			Percentage of work force		
	Electronics	Petroleum	Textiles	Electronics	Petroleum	Textiles
1967	1%	21%	3%	3%	2%	14%
1973	16%	24%	8%	22%	3%	17%
1984	23%	30%	2%	26%	2%	10%
1993	56%	10%	1%	32%	1%	7%

Figure 13.4 *The changing importance of three industries*

years, some areas of manufacturing are still outstripping it. The heavier industries such as petroleum, chemicals, paints and pharmaceuticals are expanding at only 1 to 2 per cent per annum, but electronics are expanding at 19 per cent, precision instruments at 16 per cent and machinery such as lifts and refrigerators at 12 per cent per annum.

LAND USE AND INDUSTRIAL LOCATION

The shortage of land in Singapore has given rise to great competition for space on the island between various forms of land use. Widespread reclamation schemes have increased Singapore's area by just over 10 per cent, and most of this new, flat land has been used for ports and heavy industry. Rigid structure and strategic plans produced by the government have enabled the land use patterns to be developed systematically. (Figure 13.5 shows the current pattern of land use in Singapore.)

At the time of independence, some 60 per cent of the island was agricultural; now less than 12 per cent of it is farmland, although some of this is intensive and high-tech, with such developments as

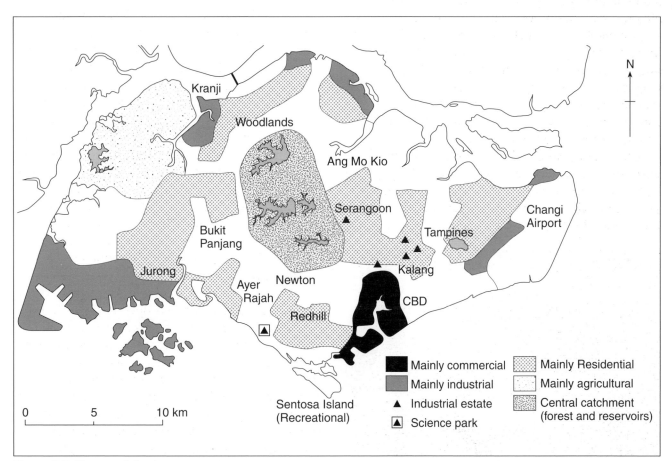

Figure 13.5 *Singapore's land use*

the industrial and economic development of Singapore

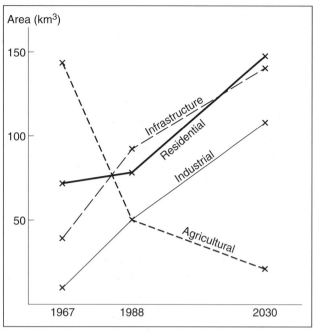

Figure 13.6 *Changing land-use patterns in Singapore*

hydroponic vegetable production. There is little need for Singapore to be self-sufficient in food production because its near neighbours have abundant land and low labour costs.

Infrastructure takes up more space in Singapore than in most countries. This reflects the importance of its harbours and Changi International Airport as a major world route centre; it also shows that the expressways (motorways) and Mass Rapid Transit system (metro) are fundamental to the island's land development strategy.

The state owned 44 per cent of the land on Singapore island at the time of independence and has now increased this to 80 per cent; this land has been acquired by the LAA (Land Acquisition Act), mainly to expand public housing. The HDB (Housing Development Board) has carried out the most spectacular change in land use by building high-rise, high-density neighbourhoods throughout Singapore. Eventually, housing will cover 25 per cent of the country's area and be able to accommodate 4 million people. Figure 13.6 shows how certain types of land use are changing within Singapore.

Industrial land use is also increasing rapidly. The biggest concentration of manufacturing industry is to the west of the CBD, close to the port of Jurong. The JTC (Jurong Town Corporation) is the leading developer and manager of industrial facilities in Singapore and runs 33 custom-built industrial estates. Heavy industries are concentrated close to the port (e.g. oil handling and refining on the newly reclaimed off-shore islands). The PSA (Port of Singapore Authority) has 15 km of quays and 600 000 m² of covered warehouses. At present the busiest port in the world by tonnage (125 600 000 tonnes in 1995), the PSA is planning to expand its container capacity four-fold between 1993 and 2018.

To overcome the problems of industrial over-concentration in the one area, the government adopted the concept of a 'Ring Plan' in 1971, to disperse industry more widely throughout the island

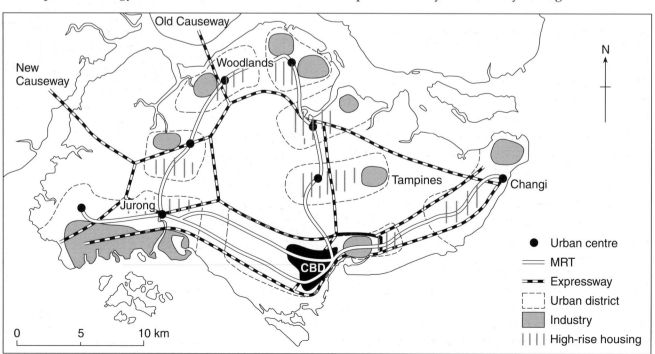

Figure 13.7 *Singapore's Ring Plan*

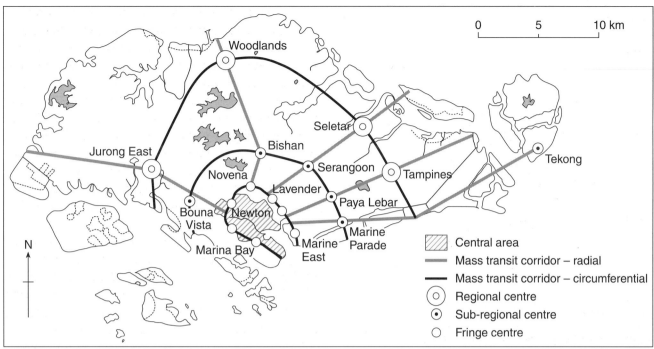

Figure 13.8 *The Constellation Plan*

(see Figure 13.7). The plan combined the spread of the expressway and MRT infrastructure, public housing neighbourhoods and new industrial estates in a comprehensive and integrated way. The basic plan was realised in the mid 1990s with the completion of the MRT northern loop through to Woodlands. With the increasing pressure upon space, the 'Ring Plan' has been modified into a denser, more complex 'Constellation Plan' (see Figure 13.8) which will give Singapore a distinctive settlement hierarchy.

INDUSTRIAL CONCENTRATION AT JURONG

Jurong was chosen as the main centre for industrial development in Singapore because of its position near the expanding port area, its proximity to the CBD and the fact that it was originally an area of unused swampland owned by the government. The setting up of the JTC enabled the Jurong Industrial Estate to be developed as an industrial agglomeration based upon a well-intergrated infrastructure. From the start, the area was divided into planned land-use zones including heavy industry, light industry, commercial and residential land and open spaces (see Figure 13.9).

Heavy industries located along the waterfront include the 21 ha site of the National Iron and Steel Mills and the Singapore Textile Industries Ltd., both state-owned enterprises which played an important role in Singapore's first period of industrialisation. The vast range of lighter industries are sited further

inland along the main highways which pass through Jurong. These industries include food processing, light engineering, printing, furniture and household goods manufacture as well as high-tech enterprises. Where there is most pressure upon space, the factories have been designed as two- or three-storey units.

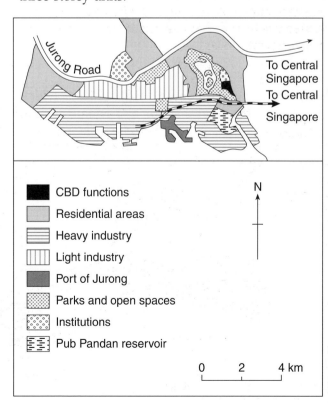

Figure 13.9 *Land use in Jurong*

the industrial and economic development of Singapore

The Jurong area now has over 1500 industrial establishments and its success in attracting Transnational Corporations has been in the government packages offered to overseas firms, which have included large tax concessions (31 per cent of profits are tax-free in the first 10 years of operation). The concentration of the high-tech industries in the Jurong area in recent years are further encouraged by its proximity to the Science Park research and development zone. Foreign TNC high-tech operators and products include: Winchester (disc drives), Philips (television components), Seagate, Micropolis and Western Digital (intergrated circuits and other microelectronics) and Hewlett Packard (calculators keyboards and printers).

PRESENT PLANNING FOR THE FUTURE

The Singapore government has a strong commitment to maintaining the country's economic power in both the secondary and tertiary sectors. How well Singapore will weather the economic storms which are currently shaking South East Asia remains to be seen.

The EBD is, at present, engaged in a number of so-called 'development thrusts' to take the Singapore economy well into the third millennium. The most important of these are:

- **Manufacturing 2000**, the aim of which is to maintain manufacturing industry at 25 per cent of the GDP and industrial employment at 20 per cent of the workforce.
- **International Business Hub 2000**, which promotes the service sector and is encouraging more businesses to locate their regional headquarters in Singapore.
- **Promising Local Enterprises (PLEs)**. Set up in 1995, this EDB scheme is to promote at least 100 new Singapore-based businesses over a ten-year period and to encourage their growth.
- **Coinvestment**. This project encourages partnerships between the PLEs and large Transnational Corporations, for both investment and risk-sharing, as PLEs often have limited financial resources.
- **Innovation Development**. Singapore has a reputation for high levels of technical and scientific education; this 'thrust' is intended to keep the country's industries competitive by being at the cutting edge of new technology through large-scale investment in R and D (Research and Development).

- **Regionalisation**. Singapore has already expanded its economic enterprises into various neighbouring countries; future plans are for much wider expansion, especially in manufacturing, to take advantage of much lower wage levels in other South East Asian countries.

SINGAPORE AS A REGIONAL ECONOMIC POWER

Singapore's economy has far outgrown its cramped island space. Reclamation schemes may provide new flat industrial and commercial sites, but room for expansion within the national frontiers is severly limited. The first major opportunity to expand came through developments within the ASEAN (Association of South East Asian Nations) regional economic organisation. The 'Growth Triangle' formed by Singapore, Johor Bahru in Malaysia and the Riau Islands in Indonesia, is an experiment in regional cooperation which had been to the benefit of all three players (see Figure 13.10). Singapore is physically linked to Johor by causeway and already has close economic ties with it when the 'Growth Triangle' concept evolved in the mid 1980s. Johor is a busy port and industrial town where new steel works and petrochemical plants are being built, together with a township for 200 000 workers. The developments on the Riau archipelago are centred on Batam Island which, although larger than

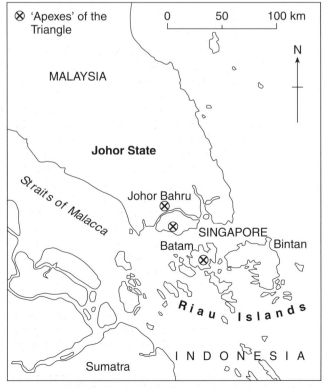

Figure 13.10 *The Growth Triangle*

Singapore, had a population of only 100 000; infrastructure has been built to support an eventual population of 700 000. Singapore has developed the Batamindo industrial estate on the island, which already has 81 companies and a workforce of 42 000. Neighbouring Bintan Island also has a small industrial estate, although its most important form of development is as a tourist resort, particularly for Singaporeans; in 1995 the new Tanah Merah Ferry Terminal was opened to link Singapore to the Bintan Beach International Resort.

The Triangle's main benefits to Singapore are space for industrial expansion and workers with much lower wages; Malaysia's per capita GNP is one-sixth of that Singapore and Indonisia's is less than one-twentieth. One of the main problems encountered has been the traditional suspicion between Malaysia and Singapore, which has made progress on cooperation rather slow. Consequently, Singapore has been busy investing in other parts of ASEAN and Asia in general.

Some of the current developments are:

● The 500 ha Vietnam-Singapore Industrial Park near Ho Chi Minh City (Saigon), inaugurated in 1996.
● Various projects in India including Singapore's first overseas Information Technology Park in Bangalore, a city with a well-educated population, launched in 1995.

Singapore hit by job losses as Asia storm bites

SINGAPORE'S boast that it would remain largely unaffected by Asia's economic storms has taken a severe knock with one of its high-tech flagships laying off workers. The city-state's second-largest employer, Seagate Technology, a US computer disk-drive maker, is dismissing 1,800 employers, about 10 percent of its workforce, and several hundred contract workers. Strong pricing stratergies by South Korean and Japanese disk-drive makers were blamed for the lay-offs, which cast a pall over trade-driven Singapore yesterday. The Government and unions were trying to find employment for those dismissed.

In this brash, super-confident city-state of three million, there is no sense of the kind of panic seen elsewhere in East Asia – no cash-strapped yuppies have committed suicide as in Thailand. But Singaporeans are bracing themselves for tougher times. Analysts agree that the financial turmoil which has brought misery to much of the region will have some effect. Tony Tan, the Singaporean Deputy Prime Minister, gave a warning this month of a possible regional recession and "temporary pains".

The traditional Chinese new year celebrations look like being low-key, with families cutting back. The market for traditional Chinese new year fare is down by as much as 20 per cent. The Year of the Tiger may come in more like a lamb. Although Singapore – one of Asia's original dragons and a regional centre for trade, transport, banking, tourism and communications – is less dramatically affected than its two larger neighbours, Indonesia and Malaysia, consumers are being more careful with their money

Singapore has fared relatively well during the six-month Asian economic meltdown, seemingly thanks to strong economic management and massive foreign reserves.

But one analyst said: "Singapore is going to be hurt as Malaysia exports less through the port here. Trade will certainly suffer and growth is going to slow across all sectors of the economy. When you add it all up, it will be quite a serious knock."

Figure 13.11 *Article from* **The Times,** *January 1998*

the industrial and economic development of Singapore

Figure 13.12 *'Little India', Singapore*

● In China, the Suzhou Industrial Park Project is Singapore's largest overseas investment. At a distance of 6 km from Shanghai and covering 70 km^2, this estate will take 20 to 30 years to complete and will employ 350 000 people.

The success of Singapore's 'Regionalism' policy can be seen in the fact that in 1996 it was the biggest foreign investor in Malaysia, the second largest in Vietnam, third in Indonesia and the Philippines, fourth in Thailand and fifth in China.

Such close ties with other Asian economies make it difficult to predict the future prosperity and success of Singapore, especially in the light of so much turbulence in the Far East in the late 1990s. However, Singapore's economy appears to be more robust because of the uniqueness of the country's position in South East Asia as well as the nature of the success tied to so many social factors such as high levels of education. A total collapse of Singapore is unlikely.

Figure 13.11 is a newspaper article which is not altogether optimistic about the situation.

SUMMARY

● Per capita GNP US $ 25 740
● Population 2.9 million
● Equatorial island of 647.5 km^2 increased by reclamation
● Important location on the Straits of Malacca, south of Malay Peninsula
● 1819 British colony; 19th century major port; 1965 independence
● Three stages of economic development; trading in raw materials; heavy manufacturing; high-tech industry and tertiary activities
● Paternalistic government: highly educated population; 80 per cent of population in public housing
● 9 per cent average growth rate over a 30-year period
● Jurong Town Corporation in charge of many industrial developments
● 'Ring Plan' for overall land-use development
● EBD in charge of six 'Development Thrusts'
● Singapore-Johore-Riau 'Growth Triangle'
● 'Regionalism' in China, India and Vietnam

EXAMINATION QUESTIONS

This case study has a much broader base than most as it deals with economic development in general, more specifically with industrialisation and even more specifically with an NIC; the case study also looks at the issue temporally as well as spatially. Thus, a wide range of answers could use information from this Singapore example.

SPECIFIC

Examples of questions dealing directly with the subject matter:

1 With reference to a country you have studied, examine the main factors which have accounted for its pattern of industrialisation.

2 Examine why the Newly Industrialised Countries (NICs)/Asian 'Tigers' have been more successful industrially than other Less Economically Developed Countries?

GENERAL

More general questions for which the case study is relevant could include development models, land-use pressures, and, as Singapore is a city state, urban planning/land use.

3 With reference to countries you have studied, examine the advantages and limitations of using theoretical models to explain their economic development.

4 What are the main conflicts of land use which may be encountered in cities which are expanding rapidly?

the industrial and economic development of Singapore

— CASE STUDY — 14
ECONOMIC CHANGE IN THE BALTIC REPUBLICS

Estonia, Latvia and Lithuania ... burst on to the world scene almost from nowhere in the late 1980s. Previously they had been, in the awareness of much of the world, almost semi-mythical places that might have existed in an old atlas or a grandparent's stamp collection.

John Noble

The three Baltic Republics, Estonia, Latvia and Lithuania, gained their independence from the disintegrating USSR at the beginning of the 1990s. The most European of the 15 republics which made up the old Soviet Union, they embarked upon policies of modernisation, democratisation and economic reform, which have enabled them to look towards the countries of Western Europe and abandon some of their heavy reliance upon Russia.

The sweeping changes have had different degrees of success in each of the three countries; all three have had problems in reorientating themselves from central planning to a free market economy. A lot of the funding for these changes has come through the London-based European Bank for Reconstruction and Development (EBRD), which was set up for the specific purpose of transforming the economies of the Central and Eastern European states that had once been Communist.

Although the Baltic Republics did not join the CIS (Commonwealth of Independent States), the vehicle whereby Russia retained most of the old member republics of the Soviet Union in a loose economic association, they still find themselves linked in one way or another to their former colonial masters. Estonia and Lativa both have large Russian minorities living within their territories, and all three still have close infrastructure links with Russia through such things as pipelines and their railway networks.

HISTORICAL BACKGROUND

Part of the great North European Plain forms the eastern seaboard of the Baltic, where the three small countries of Estonia, Latvia and Lithuania are located. Relatively flat and overlain with glacial deposits, this land of forests, farms and lakes has for millennia been open to a whole succession of waves of invaders from both west and east. Although in the last 150 years Germany and Russia have been the two main antagonists, Poles, Swedes, Danes and the Orders of the Teutonic Knights and Knights of the Sword, all subjugated local populations to their rule at various periods of time. Only Lithuania managed to establish itself as a regional power, with a much greater territory than it has now, but that was back in the 15th century.

The turbulent events of the last 200 years can explain why the Baltic Republics so strongly value their newly won independence. By the end of the 18th century the three peoples had become absorbed into the Czarist Russian Empire. The Russians tried to impose their language and culture but met stiff opposition, especially from the Lithuanians. The conflict between Germany and Russia in the First World War, together with the Russian Revolution in 1917, enabled the three Baltic Republics to fight for their independence, which Russia recognised in 1920. Independence was short lived, as the Nazis occupied the Baltic Republics in 1941. During the course of the Second World War, Estonia lost 200 000 people, Latvia 450 000 and Lithuania 475 000. In 1944, the Soviets occupied the Baltic States and Stalin embarked upon a policy of heavy industrialisation, especially in the ports, and collectivisation of agriculture; those who disagreed were either killed or deported to labour camps in Siberia. Thus Estonia lost a further 60 000 of its population, Lativa 175 000 people and Lithuania 250 000 people; these would have been mainly able-bodied members of the workforce, who were partially replaced by the large influx of Russian migrants.

By the mid 1980s, it was obvious that the Soviet economy was in a very bad state and as the USSR embarked upon its new policy of *glasnost* (openness), independence movements in the Baltic Republics took advantage of the situation. From

1988 Soviet rule was openly challenged and all three were independent by 1991; although Estonia's independence was achieved without bloodshed, people were killed in both Riga and Vilnius in struggles with Soviet troops.

All three countries have undergone rapid transformations since independence. Estonia has had the greatest success because of its strong ethnic and cultural links with Finland, which has been a major investor in its economy. The least successful has been Lithuania where political change and privatisation of state enterprises have been slowest. The rate of change in Latvia, like its geographical location, has been somewhere in between.

GEOGRAPHICAL BACKGROUND

By European standards, the Baltic Republics are small both in area and in population. Lithuania is the largest of the three, with an area of 65 200 km^2 and a population of 3.8 million; Latvia extends over 63 700 km^2, with a population of just 1.5 million. Estonia is much smaller, covering 45 200 km^2 with a population of just 1.5 million. The large-scale migrations and deportations mentioned above have left all three countries with ageing populations and, therefore, negative demographic growth rates (Estonia: –0.5

per cent per annum; Latvia: –0.7 per cent per annum; Lithuania: –0.2 per cent per annum), which is potentially bad for their economies.

ESTONIA

Made up from the mainland area together with over 800 islands, Estonia is the most northerly of the three republics. Its people are ethnically and linguistically similar to the Finns, with whom they now have very close links across the Gulf of Finland. The land is generally flat or gently undulating and underlain mainly by moraines and other glacial deposits (Figure 14.1). Where land is poorly drained, there are extensive areas of forests (which cover 48 per cent of the country), marshland and over 1500 lakes. Elsewhere, the richer soils on better drained land support a mainly pastoral economy, dominated by dairy farming.

Until the 1950s there were over 120 000 peasant smallholdings, which were forcibly collectivised during the Stalinist era into just 320 state farms. Since the early 1990s, the process of privatisation has been gradually reversing the Soviet system of landholding. The Russians also introduced heavy industry to Estonia, based on its local natural resources of bituminous shale (oil, gas, chemicals)

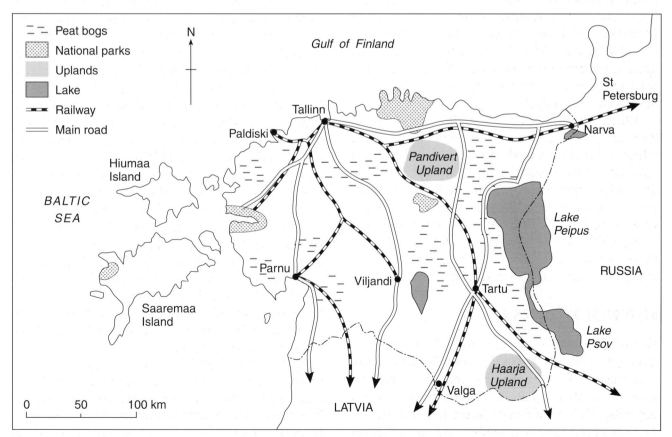

Figure 14.1 *Estonia*

and timber (paper, pulp, artifical fibres). Large-scale textile, chemical and power plants were located in the main cities and ports. At the time of industrialisation Estonians were deported and Russians brought in to replace them, leaving Estonia with a 30 per cent Russian population; the group who were once masters now find themselves a disadvantaged ethnic minority.

Figure 14.2 *The historic core of Tallinn*

The core of Tallinn, the capital of Estonia, is an architecturally rich mediaeval walled city, which is undergoing rapid restoration and transformation into an attractive tourist centre of international importance. It also continues as the country's centre of trade, commerce and industry. Investments from the EU, the EBRD and, in particular, from Finland has enabled the Estonian economy to be transformed more rapidly than that of either Latvia or Lithuania; the Estonian *kroon* was the first new Baltic currency to be introduced, when in 1992 it replaced the Russian rouble. Estonia has had the most successful programme of privatisation of industries and services of all the Baltic Republics, so much so that by 1996, only 20 large-scale enterprises were left in government hands. Joint ventures with Finnish and Swedish companies have enabled the transition to privatised industry to run smoothly, as in the case of the massive state Saku Brewery.

When Paldiski, the former Soviet nuclear base, was dismantled and handed back to the Estonians in 1995, the withdrawal of Russia was complete. However, here as elsewhere, the legacy of the old USSR has been severe enviromental degradation. The Baltic Sea around Estonia is one of the most badly polluted stretches of water in Europe and, furthermore, an estimated 30 per cent of Estonia's groundwater supplies have been contaminated by the waste from shale oil extraction. In fact, Estonia's past experience

has converted it into one of the most 'green-minded' of European states, which is developing its national park system with the aid of EBRD funds.

LATVIA

Latvia's gently undulating landscape is similar to that of Estonia, although drained by several large rivers, it has less extensive marshlands and lakes. The wooded central Vidzeme Uplands rise to over 300 m, the highest range in the Baltic Republics (Figure 14.3).

Agriculture is predominently pastoral and is, at present, undergoing privatisation with the splitting up of the Soviet-created collective farms. Latvia's main natural resources are low-value geological ones such as peat, clay, limestone and gravel, used mainly in the construction industries. Unlike Estonia, Latvia lacks fuel resources and produces only one-third of its energy need; this has meant considerable economic adjustment since the disintergration of the USSR, as Latvia relied heavily upon Russia for its coal and oil imports. Now Latvia has to buy electricity from Estonia and Lithuania, although this is not technically difficult as all three countries were on a great Soviet-wide powerline grid system. Fuel accounts for 45 per cent of the country's current imports, but following a recent agreement with the US petroleum company Amaco, it is hoped that some fossil fuel deposits will be found within Latvian territory.

Latvia, and in particular its capital Riga, was designated by Soviet state planning as a centre for specialised manufacturing which included railway rolling stock and consumer durables such as refrigerators and television sets. This has given the country a pool of skilled labour which is available for new inward investments made by foreign high-tech industries.

With a population of 900 000, Riga is the metropolis of the Baltic Republics. It has an old-world Hanseatic mediaeval core surrounded by a network of 19th-century boulevards which are lined by ornate, large buildings in eclectic styles and beyond lie the drab Soviet-era workers' flats and factories. Riga is an attractive river port city, close to numerous sandy beach resorts on the Baltic; many Russians moved to the city during the period of Soviet domination. Latvia has a Russian minority population of 34 per cent, but Riga has a Russian majority of 61 per cent. Ethnic problems are one of the country's major political and economic issues as most Russians living there do not have Latvian

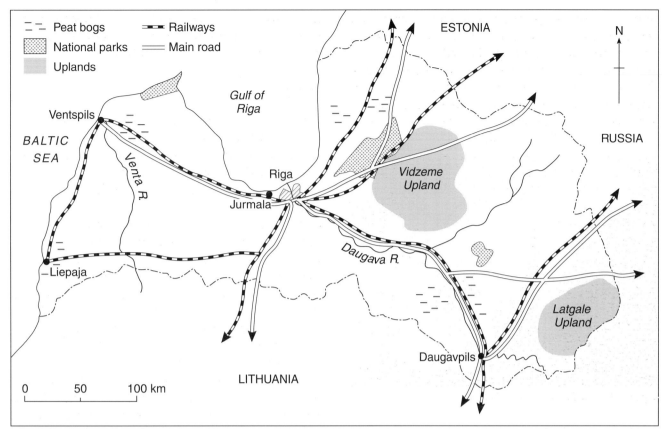

Figure 14.3 *Latvia*

Figure 14.4 *A boulevard in Riga*

nationality, yet they find the lifestyle in Riga preferable to that in Russia.

Riga and Liepaja are both ice-free ports throughout the year, unlike Tallinn or the northern Baltic Russian ports such as St Petersburg. Latvia is, therefore, deliberately taking advantage of the good infrastructural links with Moscow and developing its ports to handle Russian trade with Western Europe. So much of the future of the country does indeed depend upon keeping the balance between opening up new horizons, yet still retaining some economic links with the Russians.

LITHUANIA

Lithuania is the largest of the three Baltic Republics and, with 80 per cent of its population Lithuanian, is the most ethnically homogeneous. The country is made up of glacial lowlands in the west and more elevated and forested limestone hill country in the south and east. The coastline is dominated by the northern portion of the Courland spit, with its high sand dunes, brackish lagoon and pine and birch forests (Figure 14.5).

Lithuania is the most rural of the republics; its agriculture is predominantly pastoral, based on dairy cattle and pig rearing, but fodder crops, potatoes and rye also cover large areas of land. The structural and economic changes involved in dismantling collective farms have been much slower than in either Latvia or Estonia. Farming has relied heavily upon manual labour and the adjustments to more mechanised and commercial systems have also been slow due to the shortage of funding.

The republic has a wide range of mineral resources including gypsum, iron ore and limestone, which form the basis of some of its heavy industries. Oil has recently been discovered offshore

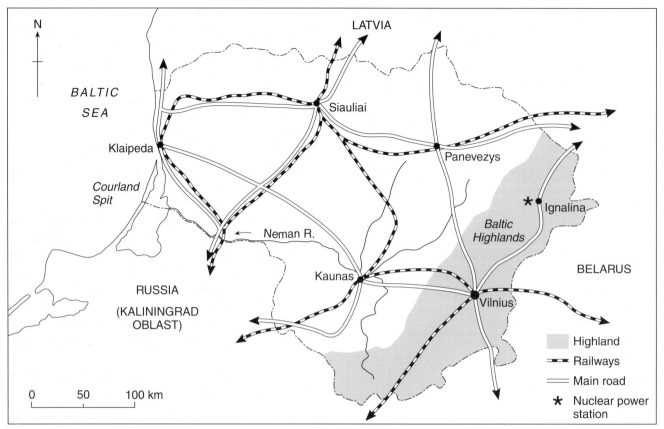

Figure 14.5 *Lithuania*

and is likely to stimulate new industrial developments. The specialist industries set up in Lithuania when part of the old USSR included shipbuilding, chemicals, cement, electrical and electronic goods. These have continued to be important since independence, but the move towards privatisation has been fairly slow; many of the politicians in power have lacked the radical reforming policies and enthusiam for foreign investment seen in either Latvia or Estonia. Indeed Lithuania does not allow foreign companies to own land, which has discouraged them from moving in and setting up manufacturing plants in the country.

As with Latvia, energy has been one of the major problems confronting independent Lithuania; 97 per cent of the country's oil has to be imported and, at present, this is mainly from Russia. Of Lithuania's electricity, 87 per cent is produced by the Ignalina nuclear power plant in the south-east of the country (originally built to be the largest in the world); this is similar to the plant at Chernobyl, which suffered the disastrous fire in 1986, and it therefore constitutes a possible threat to the people and environment. A huge EBRD loan has been granted to Lithuania to develop and extend its thermal power stations.

Figure 14.6 *The historic centre of Vilnius*

Vilnius is probably the most beautiful of the three Baltic capitals. Its historic core with its colour-washed Baroque churches, university and palaces, cobbled pedestrianised streets with bars and resturants, is a lively place which has the potential to become a major tourist destination like Prague. Although not the capital during the 1920s and the 1930s, when it was part of Poland (Kaunas was the capital during that time), Vilnius remains the main Lithuanian centre of manufacturing, services, banking and commerce.

Klaipeda, the main port of Lithuania, is located at the northern end of the Courland spit. Its handling of imports and exports for both Lithuania and its neighbours, together with its shipbuilding industry is concentrated along both the Baltic shore and within the Courland *haff* (lagoon). Offshore, a huge, deep deposit resulting from industrial pollution is poisoning the Baltic Sea; once again the legacy of unchecked heavy industry from the Soviet period threatens the health of the people of the Baltic Republics.

KALININGRAD

To the south-west of Lithuania, and sharing its long Courland spit, is what is often nicknamed 'the fourth Baltic Republic' – the Kaliningrad Oblast of the Russian Federation. This detatched exclave of Russia was a part of the German territory of east Prussia, until it was divided between the Poles and the Russians at the end of the Second World War. The German population was mainly expelled or deported and replaced by Russians.

Kaliningrad, the administrative centre, (formerly the German city of Königsberg), is now a grim and ugly post-war Stalinist-style city. Its separation from the rest of Russia has become a problem since the independence of Lithuania and the other republics. In order to take advantage of Kaliningrad's position on the Baltic, Russia has made it into a 'special economic zone' and it now attracts investment from countries such as Poland and Germany, at the same time providing Russia with an important trade outlet to Western Europe. The long, sandy beaches with their old Soviet-era resorts are also being developed as tourist attractions for foreign visitors, especially the Germans whose ties with the region go back 700 years.

THE BALTIC STATES AS TRANSITION ECONOMIES

The United Nations labels the former Communist countries of Central and Eastern Europe as 'transition economies', referring to their change from a centrally planned to a market economy. This transition is not proving to be a particularly easy one, especially for the people living in the Baltic Republics. In the Old Soviet Union, unemployment was negligible and most people had jobs for life, housing was rent free or very cheap and many basic foodstuffs were heavily subsidised. It is not surprising, therefore, that many people, especially the older generations, have suffered economically as a result of the changes and may look back to the old Soviet era as a 'golden age'.

Had the old system been perfect, it would not have collapsed. As well as a lack of political freedom, especially for the non-Russian minorities within the old USSR, the means of production was often very inefficient, promotion at work depended upon Party affiliations rather than merit and there were very few controls upon the severe impact that industry has on the physical environment and people's health.

In the transition of the Baltic economies, a great many changes have taken place. These include:

- the setting up of private banks to finance the necessary economic changes
- the establishment of private companies to set up new enterprises and to take over the running of some of the older inefficient ones
- the privatisation of some of the main state enterprises
- the restructuring of industry into more efficient units
- the development of the service sector, especially retailing, marketing, professional services, hotels, catering and tourism
- the privatisation of agriculture, re-establishing some of the pattern of the pre-1950s land ownership
- the restructuring of the transport services to suit the redrawn, post-USSR boundaries, with national bus and rail companies replacing the old Soviet infrastructure.

None of these changes would be possible without the inward investment of other European nations. It has been a special concern of the member states of the EU to stabilise the economies of the Baltic States so that their transition can be as smooth as possible. EU countries' investments in the Baltic Republics have been both bilateral (e.g. Finland in Estonia) and multilateral by operating through the EBRD in London.

Various economic and social indicators show both the processes of transition and their degree of success. All three Baltic States are finding the transition difficult and have had various political crises. High inflation, high interest rates, growing unemployment, the decline of the heavy industries, the rapid increase in the cost of living and huge trade deficits are all part of what countries undergoing economic transition have to experience. However, some of these trends are already being reversed. Figures 14.7 to 14.11 plot some of the main economic trends in recent years. Inflation rates were enormous at the start of the transition period (over 1000 per cent per annum), because of the reduction of government controls over prices, but are now getting much lower. Unemployment rates are not

particularly high in comparison with Western Europe, but are likely to increase in the future. The sectoral changes in employment are showing the continuous decline of the primary and secondary sectors in favour of the tertiary, only to be expected as countries move away from Communism and its inefficient agriculture and over-emphasis on heavy industry. Overall, the trade deficits are getting worse as the Baltic States buy more Western consumer goods and rely less upon Russian raw materials. Underlying all this, however, are fairly high GDP growth rates – some years almost on a par with the rates of the Asian 'tiger' economies.

At times the prospects may look bleak for the

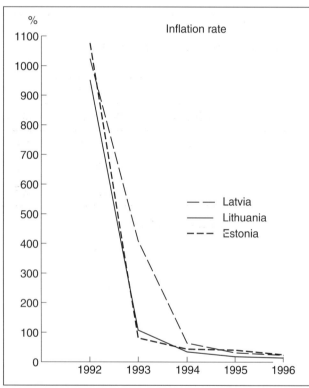

Figure 14.7 *Inflation rates*

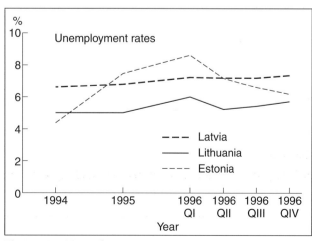

Figure 14.8 *Unemployment rates*

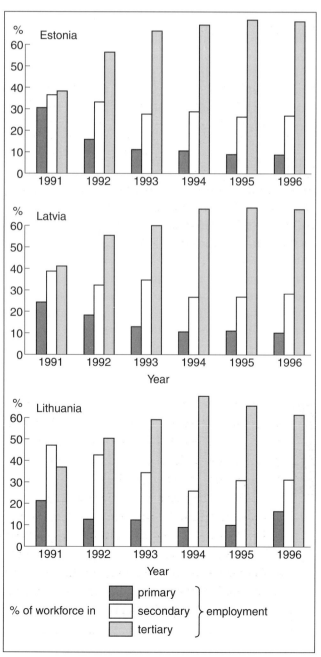

Figure 14.9 *Changes in employment structure*

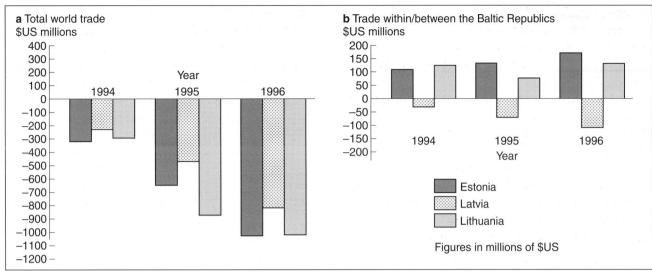

Figure 14.10 *Trade balance*

a *Total world trade*

b *Trade within/between the Baltic Republics*

Baltic Republics, but with expanding economies and re-established independence from Russian rule, there is an air of confidence especially amongst the younger generations who wish to follow the cultural trends of Western Europe. Estonia is leading the way in economic changes but the other two republics are not far behind. Within just five years of the break-up of the old Soviet Union, the Baltic States had become potential applicants for EU membership, something which would have been totally unthinkable back in the 1980s.

	% change		
	Lithuania	**Estonia**	**Latvia**
1994	1	2.8	0.6
1995	3	2.8	1.7
1996	4	3.5	2.5

Figure 14.11 *Annual growth in GDP*

SUMMARY

- Estonia, Latvia and Lithuania are small in area and population
- Frequently invaded and overrun by European powers
- Part of the Soviet Union from 1944 to 1991
- Huge economic changes since independence
- EBRD has financed many of the changes
- Latvia and Estonia still have large Russian minorities
- The transport networks are still closely linked to Russia
- Pollution is one of the great legacies of the old USSR
- Estonia has been the quickest to change, Lithuania the slowest
- Economic changes have included more trade with the West, privatisation, decollectivisation of agriculture and restructuring of industry

economic change in the Baltic Republics

●—EXAMINATION
QUESTIONS

This case study concerns development and economic change and can be used specifically to illustrate transition economies or more generally for economic development.

SPECIFIC

Specific questions could include:

1 What is meant by a transition economy? With reference to specific examples, examine the changes which are taking place in transition economies today.

2 With reference to a country or countries you have studied, account for the changes which are taking place to former centrally planned economies.

GENERAL

More general economic questions could include:

3 Critically assesss the contention that there is no longer such a thing as the 'Third World'.

4 What criteria would you use to assess countries' levels of development? Illustrate your answer with examples of countries with differing types of economy.

— CASE STUDY — **15** NATURE TOURISM IN COSTA RICA

Sustainability and ecotourism are words on the lips of all Costa Ricans, from the rich entrepreneurs to the *campesinos* (peasant farmers) who struggle to make a living in the remotest corners of the country ...

Marco Linda, 'Ecotourism in Costa Rica,' L'Universo

The seven countries of Central America (see Figure 9.1) have tremendous potential for tourism. They have a rich environmental and cultural heritage which includes tropical rainforests with unique fauna, active volcanoes, unspoilt coastlines, coral reefs, pre-Colombian archaeological sites and historic colonial cities. Yet most of these countries have had severe political problems and Guatemala, Nicaragua, Panama and El Salvador, in particular, have suffered from instability in the last few decades, which has rendered them poor in comparison with other parts of the Western Hemisphere and has inhibited the development of tourism. (Figure 15.1 shows the GNP and the tourist arrivals for the seven countries.)

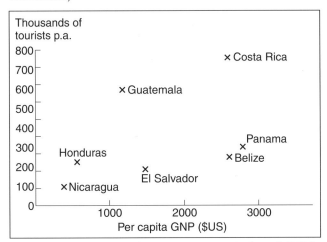

Figure 15.1 *Relationship between tourist arrivals and GNP in Central America*

Costa Rica and Belize stand out from the other countries in two ways:

● they have both been politically stable for a long time
● they have encouraged tourism to develop along sustainable 'ecotourism' lines.

The success of tourism in these two countries brings into question just what is meant by sustainability and if there should be a limit to the number of tourists visiting specific places. Although their tourist infrastructures are less developed, countries such as Honduras and Nicaragua are trying to emulate the success of Costa Rica and to copy its model by developing nature tourism.

COSTA RICA'S ECONOMIC AND POLITICAL BACKGROUND

Costa Rica has two striking features:

● it has one of the lowest expenditures on armaments in the world
● it has one of the largest percentages of its land under environmental protection.

These two factors are not unrelated, but suggest that Coast Rica has rather different priorities from most other nations.

This small Central American republic with an area of 51 032 km² and a population of 2.9 million, gained its independence from Spain in 1821. Its main economic specialisation was initially coffee and, during the 19th century, large areas of virgin forest in the Central Valley were given by the government to the coffee planters for clearance. Throughout the 20th century Costa Rica remained politically stable, apart from two short periods (1917–19 and 1948). A new constitution drawn up in 1949 abolished the armed forces and Costa Rica managed to thrive at a time when most of its neighbours were involved in internal armed struggles. In the 1980s the President, Oscar Arias, acted as a negotiator between the rival factions in neighbouring countries, for which he was given the 1987 Nobel Prize for Peace.

In the 1990s, the region has concentrated on trade rather than political struggles and the CACM (Central American Common Market), by strengthening the trading ties between countries, has enabled Costa Rica to diversify its economy.

However, like so many Latin American countries, Costa Rica still has a large foreign debt (partly because of a sharp decline in world coffee prices) and has a balance of payments deficit which fluctuates between US $ 200 and $ 500 million per annum.

The country has a high standard of living in comparison with its neighbours, yet with a high population growth rate of 2 per cent per annum adding to its economic problems, tourism is becoming increasingly important as an earner of foreign exchange. Figure 15.2 shows how the fortunes of the country's three main income earners are changing in relation to one another. The huge additional influx of tourists into Costa Rica in the decade 1984–94 (from 273 901 to 761 468) represents an increase of 16 per cent per annum. A WWF survey records that 87 per cent of visitors travel to Costa Rica for its natural environment and 52 per cent of all tourists considered themselves to be 'ecotourists'.

Of Costa Rica's territory, 27 per cent is protected by law and forms a network of 63 National Parks and other types of nature reserve (see Figure 15.3).

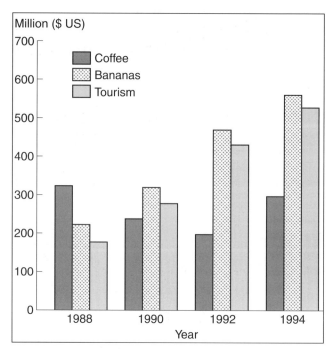

Figure 15.2 *Costa Rica's three main income earners*

Just 12 per cent of the nation's original forest cover remains today, mainly in these protected areas.

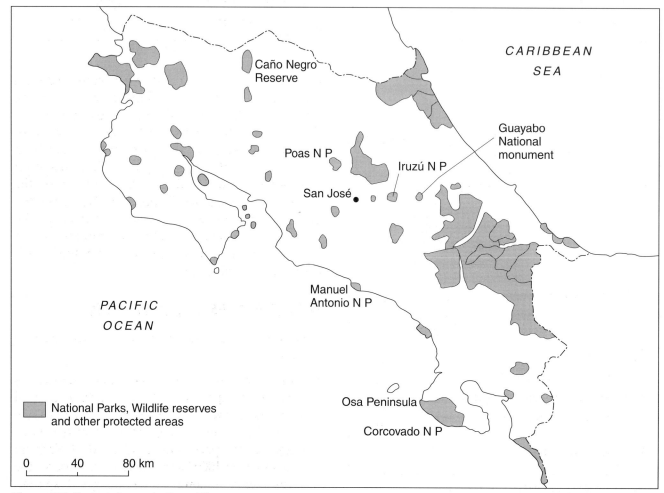

Figure 15.3 *Protected areas in Costa Rica*

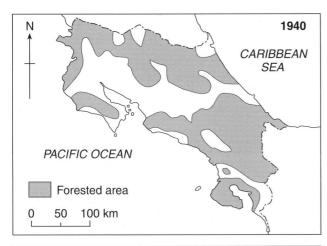

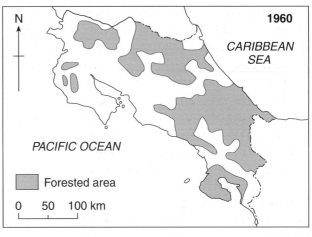

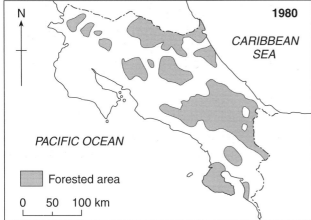

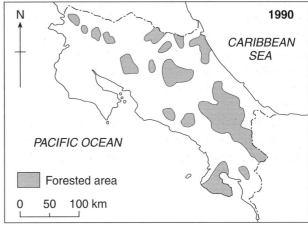

Figure 15.4 *Decline of forest cover in Costa Rica*

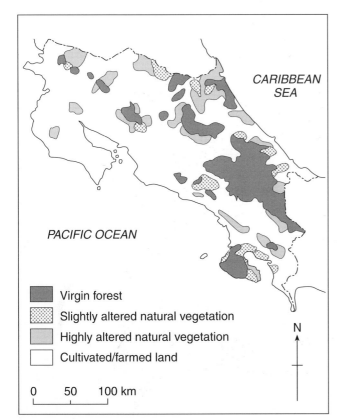

Figure 15.5 *Changes to natural vegetation*

Despite the government's attitude to conservation, a lot of damage has been done since the 1930s, especially in the Central Valley, where 60 per cent of the population live. Figure 15.4 illustrates the rate of deforestation since 1940. Not only has there been deforestation but, in many places, there has been considerable modification and alteration of the original forest type (see Figure 15.5). Neverless, the great attraction of Costa Rica is its biodiversity; the country occupies only 0.003 per cent of the Earth's land surface, yet it contains 4 per cent of the Earth's plant and animal species.

THE NATIONAL PARKS AND RESERVES

There are various categories of protected areas in Costa Rica.

- *Parques Nacíonales* (National Parks). These are 19 areas with special and outstanding natural environments which are generally home to a wide range of flora and fauna, some of which may be unique to the particular location. Most National Parks are over 1000 ha in extent. They preserve the natural environments and endangered species;

within them hunting, the building of hotels and the introduction of non-indigenous species are forbidden. The parks have numerous information and educational facilities.

● *Riservas Biológicas* (Biological Reserves). These eight reserves are run by the National Parks administration and are areas of important flora and fauna, although they may not have the scenic beauty of the National Parks. They attract visitors who are particularly interested in the wildlife the reserves harbour.

● *Rifugios Naciónales de Vida Silvestre* (Wildlife Refuges). These nine refuges are administered by the Wildlife Department to preserve the habitats of endangered species, their size depending on the nature of the habitat. Mainly of interest to scientists, the refuges also attract some ecotourists.

● *Riservas Indigenas* (Resources reserves for the indigenous peoples). Run by the Forestry Department, these 22 reserves conserve natural resources, mainly forests, for the traditional uses made by indigenous people of the areas and for possible future developments. Such reserves, unlike National Parks, are not major tourist destinations.

● **National Monument** (archaeological site).

● **Miscellaneous state-protected areas**. There are three of these, including two research stations.

● Outside of the state network, there are an increasing number of **private reserves** which act as both research and conservation centres as well as part of the nature tourist infrastructure. The most important of these is the Monteverde Cloud Forest Reserve.

EXAMPLES OF NATIONAL PARKS

The nature of the development of Costa Rica's National Parks and the threats upon them can be seen by contrasting two such parks, the Manuel Antonio and the Corcavado. The former is small and accessible, the latter is large but remote.

Costa Rica is a mountainous country which experiences heavy tropical downpours during the rainy season. This means that travel by road is generally slow and often journeys may be interrupted; it also helps to explain why 75 per cent of tourists visit only the four most accessible National Parks: Torteguero, a turtle breeding area, and Cahuita where there is a fine coral reef, both on the Caribbean coast; Poas, the volcano in the Central Valley; and Manuel Antonio on the Pacific coast. For those making only a short visit to Costa Rica, these parks are easily accessible by road; internal flights are expensive and this adds to the inaccessibility of certain more remote locations.

Manuel Antonio (see Figure 15.6) is the smallest National Park in the network, comprising a mere 682 ha of protected land. It is only 132 km from the capital, San José, although the journey may take over 4 hours on an express bus because of the disrepair of the mountain roads. The park is made up of a combination of a series of rocky coves, sandy beaches, a small coral reef and forest-clad headlands. Created a National Park in 1972, it was destined to become an international luxury resort complex, when the government compulsorily bought the land

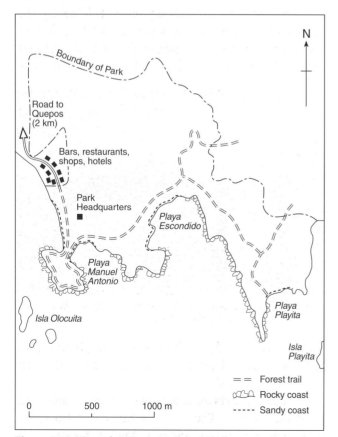

Figure 15.6 *Manuel Antonio National Park*

Figure 15.7 *The coastline at Manuel Antonio National Park*

Figure 15.8 *Monkeys in the Manuel Antonio National Park*

from a French developer. Two kilometres from the park is the bustling, rapidly growing port of Quepos, where there are many locally run budget guest houses, and on the road between Quepos and the National Park the more exclusive luxury hotels are sited. Within the park no buildings are allowed other than the rangers' headquarters and information offices; however, just outside the park there are numerous local enterprises, including bars, restaurants and gift shops.

Manuel Antonio, despite its size, is extremly biodiverse and represents the last remaining area of forest of its type in that part of Cost Rica. It has 138 species of tree, over 350 species of bird, some of them rare, 99 species of mammal including sloths, ant-eaters, monkeys, ocelots and foxes, and reptiles including iguanas and ctenosaur lizards.

Although the foreign ownership of the park area and the possible resort development are both in the past and now many local people are involved in providing services for the 'eco-' and other types of tourists, there are some social elements who are more marginalised and have resorted to petty theft from visitors to the area. However, Manuel Antonio and Quepos have a low crime rate and are safe areas for tourists, in comparison with other parts of Latin America.

There are some signs of slight environmental changes brought about by the pressure of visitors in such a small protected area. Despite warnings about how to treat the wildlife, people are feeding the monkeys which leads to behavioural changes, and some of the larger lizards are becoming more aggressive as a result of human intrusion upon their habitat. Another detrimental effect of the pressure of tourism is the erosion of trail pathways, some of which now have to be closed off for repairs.

The Corcovado National Park is one of the most remote in Costa Rica, being located on the Osa

Peninsula on the Pacific coastline, some 330 km to the south-east of San José. A poor, rough road links it to the capital, making the journey time 10 to 12 hours.

Covering 41 788 ha, it is the most biodiverse of all the parks with more than 1000 species of tree, 140 species of mammal, 177 species of reptile, 337 species of bird and at least 6000 different varieties of insect. Species which particularly attract tourists include scarlet macaws, pumas, peccaries (wild pigs), tapirs, crocodiles and caimans. This tropical wildlife haven is large enough for visitors to travel a long way from civilisation on two- or three-day treks along well-marked trails.

Corcovado is not only rich in wildlife but also in minerals, especially gold. Although the park was established in 1976, gold prospecting and panning has been taking place on the Osa Peninsula since the 1930s, where there are 39 mineral concession zones for working the gold. Both Costa Rican and international mineral companies have interests in the area. The biggest point of conflict for the Corcovado park has been the *oreros*, the peasant communities who live precariously from panning the gold and working it into ornaments for sale. The *oreros* have little respect for the demands of conservation and were found to be working inside the park boundaries; subsequently evicted by the authorities, these poor, marginalised Costa Ricans remain resentful of the changes that are taking place in the area. Only a few have latched on to the new

Figure 15.9 *Poor housing at Quepos on the edge of the Manuel Antonio National Park*

'green gold' which can be made through acting as forest guides and displaying their traditional crafts to the 'ecotourists'.

Similar conflicts exist between the *campesinos* and local authorities. The peasant farmers who grow subsistence crops in clear areas of forest on a traditional 'slash and burn' basis are also making incursions into the National Park territory. There people, who are poor and often displaced from other parts of the country, feel thay are missing out on the economic developments which arise from tourism; once again, only the more enterprising manage to get involved in the 'green tourist boom'.

Yet another threat to the Corcovado park comes from other types of tourist developments. Along the coast to the north of the park is Bahia Drake, which is being developed as a luxury resort mainly for the upper end of the United States tourist market. This resort, although 18 km away, is having a big impact by increasing the number of day trippers to the park, frequently people with little ecological interest; it also threatens to change the attitude of the local population in terms of what foreign tourists expect and the way in which the natural environment is being exploited.

THE CONCEPT OF SUSTAINABLE TOURISM

Sustainability of tourism is the ability of tourism to continue at present levels or, indeed, increase its operations to incorporate larger numbers of visitors to a region. Three main factors influence sustainability:

1 How the country or region is perceived by potential visitors and by travel industry. Places go in and out of fashion according to where they are in the 'tourism product life-cycle'. For Costa Rica, there are no problems as it is an area of rapid growth for the tourist industry.
2 The political stability of the country. Revolutions, coups, terrorist attacks and civil wars may all lead to the quick withdrawal of tourist operators and the collapse of the whole tourist industry. Again, Costa Rica currently has no problems in sustaining its tourism as it is, with Belize, the most stable of the CACM countries.
3 The environmental changes which are taking place as a result of tourism. This is particularly pertinent for 'ecotourism', with which too many tourists could destroy the very things they visit a country to experience.

Only one detailed study has been carried out in Costa Rica to determine the degree of sustainability in a specific location. The Guayabo National Monument in the centre of the country, although not a National Park, has large tracts of natural forest vegetation with nature trails. Covering an area of 217 ha, it is smaller than even the Manuel Antonio park and receives some 12 500 visitors per year; over 90 per cent of these are Costa Ricans as the archaeological zone is of great national importance in a country which lacks the huge pre-Colombian city ruins found elsewhere in Central America.

The study set out to discover what the actual 'carrying capacity' (i.e. the total number of visitors) of the area would be without causing environmental degradation. Calculations took into account group sizes, numbers of groups and the distances between them. Three levels of results were produced:

1 The 'physical' carrying capacity – the total number of visitors the environment could withstand during the course of a year: 2.7 million.
2 The 'real' carrying capacity – the physical carrying capacity adjusted to take into account limiting environmental factors such as rainfall, erosion and landslides: 1 million.
3 The 'effective' carrying capacity – the real carrying capacity with human organisational factors taken into account (e.g. the availability of park guides): 266 950.

Even the lowest of these projections shows that Costa Rica has a long way to go before it reaches tourist saturation point; however, there are also many qualitative aspects of pressure resulting from large numbers of visitors which need to be taken into account.

CRITICISMS OF NATURE TOURISM

The success of ecotourism has inevitably led to widespread criticism, both of its value in preserving the environment and in the misuse of the term; such observations may apply equally to world trends in general and to specific situations in Costa Rica.

The current wisdom of certain geographers involved with tourism issues is that it is much better for people to go to already overcrowded and overdeveloped resort areas such as Ibiza and Corfu than to the wilderness regions of the world, as it would cause less damage to the natural environment. However, such extreme suggestions, if followed, would be disastrous for the economy of countries specialising in ecotourism, such as Costa Rica.

More radical criticisms have suggested that ecotourism merely wishes to impose 'Western' values upon other societies, depriving them of their traditional livelihoods through conservation of the natural environments that attract foreign tourists. The organisation, Survival International, which fights for the rights of tribal peoples throughout the world, tries to put these issues into perspective.

The problems and criticisms surrounding ecotourism are not just about environmental degradation, but also degradation of the term. Ecotourism is an excellent concept, but the term is becoming overused by people and organisations which want to cash in on its success.

The conflict is really between the genuine, 'green' local operators and the bigger organisations which see ecotourism as a major profit-making investment. Tourism Concern, an organisation which scrutinises the way in which tour companies promote themselves, is particularly involved in such issues. Genuine ecotourism should satisfy three basic requirements:

1   It should protect the local environment and not cause degradation.
2   It should help the local population by increasing their standard of living and, by meeting local people, promote mutual understanding.
3   It should provide what is required by a growing number of specialist tourists.

In Costa Rica these demands are generally being met, but there are conflicts brought about by national organisations. For example, on the one hand INBio (Costa Rica's Institute for Biodiversity), is researching throughout the country to build up a data bank of all species that need to be preserved, whereas on the other, the *Fundación Neotrópical* promotes the use of forest resources in such a way that on the Osa Peninsula near the Corcovado National Park 600 000 tonnes of timber are exploited each year.

More disturbing are the tourist developments sponsored by national and international corporations which use the 'green' label. One example of this is the 'Papagayo Ecodevelopment' at Calubra Bay on the Costa Rican Pacific coast. The development will include more than 1000 homes, 6000 condominium flats, over 6500 hotel rooms, a golf course and a shopping complex. This US-style resort will bring profits to wealthy Costa Ricans and international tour operators rather than the locals, and certainly will have nothing to do with the spirit of ecotourism.

SUMMARY

- Ecotourism as a concept
- Stability of Costa Rica
- 761 468 annual visitors to Costa Rica
- 27 per cent of territory protected
- 19 National Parks
- Different types of protected area

- 60 per cent of population in Central Valley
- 12 per cent of nation's forests still remain
- Manuel Antonio smallest park, 682 ha
- Corcovado, more remote, 41 788 ha
- Concept of carrying capacity
- Conflicts between peasant farmers and conservation

 EXAMINATION QUESTIONS

This case study can operate at three levels: tourism in general, ecotourism in more specific terms and on a much broader scale, economic development in LEDCs.

GENERAL

Questions that may involve wider application of the case study:

3   With reference to places you have studied, examine the increasing role of tourism in the economies of LEDCs.
4   Assess the advantages and disadvantages of tourist developments in specific areas you have studied.

SPECIFIC

Specific questions relating to the case study:

1   With reference to countries you have studied, examine what is meant by ecotourism and assess how successful it has been.
2   With reference to specific examples, examine the threat and competition over land use which may be found in protected areas such as National Parks.

HOW TO CHOOSE, USE AND REVISE CASE STUDIES

CHOOSING CASE STUDIES

When making the choice of which case study to use in answering a particular examination question, there are several considerations to be made, generally concerning its appropriateness. The most important points to consider are:-

- **Is it at the right scale? A careful check is needed here as to the wording of the question. Is the example or case study required at a local, regional or continental scale? If it is at the wrong scale, the candidate will be penalised.**
- **Is the required case study for an MEDC or an LEDC? When under examination pressure, it is easy for a candidate to make a mistake in misidentifying a country or region from the point of view of its level of development. Sometimes questions require two contrasting countries or regions and in such cases it is best to take one from an MEDC and the other from an LEDC.**
- **Does the case study have the right characteristics? If a large city is under discussion, the chosen case study should be large enough to cover the required criteria. If an area of coastal deposition is asked for by the question an area which is predominently erosional should not be chosen as the representative case study. Although these two examples may be stating the obvious, candidates very frequently get themselves into trouble by selecting inappropriate material which then makes it difficult to develop their answers properly. The selection of wrong case study material can also lead to a lot of irrelevant information being written down for which very few marks can be awarded.**

It may indeed be difficult to have a few case studies which are likely to cover all needs for all potential questions. What is important, however, is for the candidate to know how to use the various case studies at his disposal to the best effect.

USING CASE STUDIES

Different types of questions will require case studies to be used in different ways. If an entire question has to be centred around just one case study, then it needs to be planned much more carefully. The answer needs to be broken down into sections, and for each section there needs to be careful interspersing of general arguments and geographical principles with exemplar material from the case study. The function of the case study in such a question is back up the candidate's opinions or arguments to prove whether or not some basic principles or patterns are true or false in the experience of specified places.

Where contrasting case studies are called for then the approach is quite similar, and the chosen case studies should enable a candidate to bring out strong contrasts in order to prove or disprove a basic geographical principle or the existence of some basic spatial patterns.

The third important use of case studies is in examination questions where they are not directly demanded by the question yet are highly relevant to the topic. Here the candidates must be careful not to go into too much detail and in particular not to go off at a tangent, thereby not answering the question; it is all too easy to 'show off' one's knowledge, but this does not get extra marks if it does not serve to address the question in hand. The prime use of case studies when not being dealt with in depth is to provide place names, statistics and other information which can briefly back up arguments or shine light upon a particular topic under discussion.

REVISING CASE STUDIES

Case studies contain a great deal of factual material, statistics and place names as well as technical terms, all of which are important to remember to use in an examination answer. Revision of so much detailed material can be a daunting task. The more theoretical parts of an A Level syllabus, such as models, are in general easier to commit to memory through revision, yet it is just the type details contained within a study which may separate out an 'A' grade answer from a lower grade answer. The key to good revision is to develop a system which makes it easy to commit detailed material to memory.

Each of the case studies has a summary box after it; this is just one way in which the information can be reduced to a simplified form, which can then be memorised fairly easy. The flow chart at the end of Case Study 7 is another good way of summarising the material. Not only does this method make the main points in the chapter easy to remember, but also enables students to understand and clarify interrelationships between the various factors involved in the study. Students should be encouraged to develop their revision skills by formulating their own flow charts and summary boxes. Another good method of revising detailed information is to prepare a revision sheet for each topic and/or subtopic (e.g on the Japanese river regimes case study, the actual regimes and how they are distributed throughout Japan would count as a subtopic, whereas the whole chapter would count as the topic). The revision sheet could ideally be subdivided into sections using the following headings:

- **Main points. This would select the most important theoretical concepts in the case study, make each into a short phrase, listing and numbering them.**

- **Technical terms. Listing the important geographical terms in the chapter, including foreign terms where necessary, and giving definitions where needed.**

- **Place names. It is important to learn place names and to spell them correctly; it all helps to distinguish a good answer from a poor one.**

- **Statistics. List the most relevant figures which can then give power to your arguments. This will make an answer stand out in comparison to a vague and washy statement with no statistics.**

- **Maps and diagrams. So often examination answers lack good, clear maps or diagrams. These can often summarise so much in a short space, which might take several paragraphs in words. (Examiners often comment on the reluctance of candidates to use graphical material to illustrate A Level answers.)**

INDEX